The

SH!T

NO ONE TELLS YOU
ABOUT BABY #2

A Guide to Surviving Your Growing Family

DAWN DAIS

SEAL PRESS

ISBN 978-1-58005-631-1

Library of Congress Cataloging-in-Publication Data is available.

Published by
SEAL PRESS
An imprint of Perseus Books
A Hachette Book Group company
1700 Fourth Street
Berkeley, California
Sealpress.com

Cover Design: Kimberly Glyder
Interior Design: Megan Jones Design
Interior Illustrations: Dawn Dais

Printed in the United States of America

10 9 8 7 6 5 4 3 2 1

To Daniel, for completing our little family

Contents

INTRODUCTION

WELCOME, DEAR READERS! I'm so happy to be writing another *Sh!t* book full of entertainment and information. Although it seems that none of us are big on actually retaining information because this book is about adding another baby to the family. Please see my first *Sh!t* book, *The Sh!t No One Tells You: A Guide to Surviving Your Baby's First Year*, for about two hundred pages of reasons why we probably should have thought this through a little more. Babies are not for the faint of heart.

It happens to the best of us, this thought that we are ready for another child. Our firstborn gets a little bigger, and maybe a little easier. Last week, Child #1 might have actually let you have two full nights of sleep (not two nights in a row; that's crazy talk). He or she might be walking and talking and generally becoming an actual little person.

That is so exciting! You know what would be even more exciting? If there were more little people!

And so here we are. You are either thinking about acquiring more little people, are in the process of acquiring one, or maybe you already have a new baby and are seeking comfort after realizing that this has all gotten out of hand. Any way you look at it, there will be shit hitting a fan in your near future.

And wherever there is parenting shit, I am there to help. Because I'm looking out for you, dear readers. We all have our callings in life; mine just involves grown women being mentally unraveled by tiny people.

By the time your second child comes along, you may feel that you have a handle on this parenting gig. Or at least a hell of a better grasp than you had the first go-round. Granted, that's not saying much because there is a good possibility that your baby knowledge before you had your first kid consisted entirely of what you'd gleaned from Johnson & Johnson commercials, those *Look Who's Talking* movies, and that one time you held that one baby. So there was more than a little room for growth.

This time around, you are a wealth of parenting knowledge (although you still find those *Look Who's Talking* movies to be quite informative), and you are more than ready for a new baby. At least that's what you think.

Although I believe a healthy dose of delusion is a necessary part of parenting, it's also important for you to realize that my shit-hitting-fan metaphor above is a much more accurate representation of parenting multiple children than anything you've posted to your "Baby #2!" Pinterest board.

As we head off on this new adventure together, I want to prepare you for the reality that you can pin to your "I've Lost Control of the Situation" board. This reality has a lot of ups and downs, good news and bad news.

GOOD NEWS: You now have a lot of experience taking care of a baby.

BAD NEWS: You have a lot of experience taking care of *one* baby. This new baby won't do anything the same way as your first baby because that would be too easy. And babies aren't in the business of making anything easy, ever.

GOOD NEWS: Your heart will never be more full than when both of your children are laughing at the same time.

BAD NEWS: You will never question your entire existence more than when both of your children are crying at the same time.

GOOD NEWS: Your kids may be best friends someday.

BAD NEWS: That day will most likely be years after they move out of your house.

So, as you can see, there are so many good times ahead!

This book has a screaming baby on the front, but I have exciting news! The screaming actually extends well beyond baby-hood and will continue for the majority of the childhood years. (You'll be so excited when they *finally* start giving you the silent treatment as teenagers.)

We are going to cover welcoming a new baby into your home in this book, but we are also going to expand into the joy that is having two mobile/talking children in your home. Let this book be a constant reminder to never let your guard down as your kids grow from babies to toddlers to preschoolers and beyond. Because the bigger they grow, the better they will get at working together to break you. Considering you haven't slept in years and you have the corresponding mental acuity, this is not a difficult undertaking for your energized children. Also—and this is more bad news—their brains are getting stronger each day, while yours is at the point at which you spent three minutes last night trying to remember the word "strawberry."

The only real hope you have against your growing child army and their expanding brains is to make sure you are constantly building up your own defenses. We all know you can't do this alone (and now that you have multiple children, you don't actually get to do anything alone ever again). That's where mom friends come in.

Mom friends are always there to offer a supportive sounding board, tips on how to tame your feral animals, and complete understanding as to why you can't remember the word "strawberry" (although don't count on them to actually help you remember anything; their brains are just as fried as yours).

Once again I've enlisted my own mom friends to provide their opinions and insights into the cluster-f that is parenting multiple children. They are my *Moms on the Front Lines*, and they are here to tell their tales of terror from the battlefields. Their stories and advice (and general *I feel you, girl*) can be found throughout the book. You can never have too many good mom friends ("good" being light on judgment and perfection and heavy on wine and humor), and I'm glad to have mine along for another peek into our collective parenting pain.

So let's head out together on our next adventure: Baby, Take Two.

There will be struggles and tears, freak-outs and fruit snacks, advanced acrobatics and juggling. And that's just your effort to get out the damn door on time.

You're gonna need some protective gear. That fan is about to turn on.

MY MOMS ON THE FRONT LINES

*T*HERE IS A shorthand that exists between moms. You can get three words into describing a harrowing parenting moment, and they are already nodding their heads, knowing where this story is going. They know why you are wearing the same pants you had on the last time they saw you. They understand why your child might not be wearing anything at all when they come over to your house. They agree that a trip to the grocery store alone sounds like a solid way to spend a Friday night.

The deeper I get into this parenting journey, the more I value the simplicity of mom friends. There is no need to go into great detail about your various hiccups along the way because they are hiccupping right along with you. They just get it. They often offer advice, but mostly they give you the good old, "Me too" that helps you tackle another day of herding children.

My merry band of mom friends is once again on board to help you navigate the myriad of parenting challenges you will face when the little people in your house start multiplying. My Moms on the Front Lines (or MOFL, as I refer to them throughout the book) have been in the trenches with multiple children and are here to offer you their hard-earned wisdom and expertise. But more important, they are here to share their stories and provide a collective "Me too."

Many moms have contributed throughout the book. Here are the names you'll see pop up most often. I asked them to give you their stats and also any quick piece of advice they wanted to share.

ME, DAWN: We have two kids, Vivian, age five, and Daniel, age three. My uterus and my brain cannot fathom the thought of any more children, so our family is complete. My partner, Becky, and I have been together nine years, and we both work part-time to full-time from home. We also share our home with two dogs and two cats because it's important to us that we constantly have a living being near or on us at all times of the day and night.

AMY: I'm a thirty-eight-year-old math and science teacher with two girls: Carly (seven) and Rory (four). I've been married to Jon for more than thirteen years. My advice to moms out there: Try to spend time with your kids while they still want to spend time with you. And don't buy Calico Critters or Shopkins.

BROOKE: We've been married six years and have two kids, a five-year-old girl and a boy who is three. I previously worked full-time, then part-time after the first baby, and now I am at home full-time. My husband works from home two to three days a week and travels overnight at least once a week. We are done with kids!!

CARRIE: I'm thirty-six years old and have been married for eight years. I have two sons, ages six and four. I work full-time in the hospitality industry. Enjoy, hug, and love them every day. As they say, time really does go fast.

DANA: We've been married for ten years. We have one girl (five years old) and one boy (three years old). Both my husband and I work full-time (or more). We are lucky to have family that live close by to help with our demanding schedules—in addition to our daycare provider, whom I consider my children's second mom and part of the family. She loves them like her own and is vital to our ability to function as a family the way we do!

DEANNA: We've been married eleven years. We have three kids: eight, five, and three. We both work full-time. We are done having kids. Advice? Laugh and remember they are only little for a short time.

DEBBIE: I've been married for twelve years, we have five kids, and I work part-time. My kids are twenty-two, eighteen, ten, seven, and four.

JEN: I'm thirty-eight and *trying* to be divorced. My kids are five and seven years old. I work full-time, go to school full-time, and I'm full-time crazy (*crazy* defined as sleep-deprived, super-stressed-out, can't think straight, loving mom).

JILL: I'm married with ten-year-old boy/girl twins. I stayed at home until the kids started first grade and then went back to teaching full-time. My advice is to always make time for each kid and for yourself as parents! They will grow up quickly, so enjoy every moment! (And always have a beer on hand.)

KAYSEE: I've been married nine years. We have three kids: one boy, age eight, and two girls, ages six and a half and three. We own a business, and I work very part-time and spend most of my time being a mommy.

MICHAELA: I've been married for five years. We have one three-year-old boy and a one-year-old girl. Two kids and done . . . plus the wild, lunatic dog we love, but who is as much work as the toddler. Brad and I both work full-time.

MICHELLE: I'm a thirty-four-year-old stay-at-home-mom. My boys are five and three years old. My husband and I have been married ten years. I previously worked part-time and am loving staying at home. Taking time for myself and connecting on date nights definitely helps everyone stay happy!

MONICA: We have four kids, ages eleven, nine, five, and three. The three-year-old keeps me as busy as my other children combined! I'm a stay-at-home mom; I drive a minivan. . . . That pretty much sums it all up in one sentence. I *still* wouldn't have it any other way. Maybe by the next book I'll be on number 5 . . .

SARAH B.: We have two boys (six and three), one dog (nine), two cats (seventeen and fifteen), and one tortoise (fiftyish)! We have been married ten years but have been together over twenty years. We both work full-time. My advice is to try to be present and enjoy the moment. Chores can wait. They grow so fast. (This is more like advice to myself.)

SARAH G.: We've been married sixteen years; we both work full-time. We employ a village to help care for our kids and keep the household running. We have four kids, ages twelve, nine, five, and two.

THE SH!T NO ONE TELLS YOU ABOUT BABY #2

YOU ARE ABOUT TO ABANDON YOUR FIRSTBORN

1

This will come up in therapy later

PROCEED WITH CAUTION

I'm telling you, it's all downhill after they make you pose holding the ultrasound. Don't do it!

*Y*OUR POOR FIRST baby has no idea what is coming, and life has not prepared them for this transition. This child has been the center of the universe for quite a while now, and you are about to break the most unfortunate news regarding the population of said universe. And you are going to have to break the news in the most unfortunate way.

No matter how much you try to explain the concept of a new baby, your firstborn won't really appreciate the reality of the situation until that damn thing comes through the front door. Even then, it may take a few days for it to really sink in that this little alien-looking thing isn't going away anytime soon. In fact, it appears as though everyone thinks the alien lives here now. Something has clearly gone terribly wrong.

And just like that, the Golden Child has been toppled from the throne.

Your firstborn will have some thoughts on another child coming into the home. And those thoughts will go a little something like this:

This is some bullshit.

It all started out as so much fun. How was I supposed to know what was coming? I got a new baby doll and a new Big Kid bed in a new Big Kid room. I even got to pick out a new comforter. Who doesn't love a new comforter? I also got some cute new shirts with things written on them that I couldn't actually read. But Mom loved taking pictures of me wearing the shirts, so I went along with it. She and I have always disagreed about the level of excitement that clothes warranted, so why was I to believe these outfits were any different?

Let this be a lesson to all of you that you should never trust anything you can't actually read. Especially if someone else seems overly excited about whatever it says. Some of us have had to learn this lesson the hard way.

Looking back on it now, I probably should have asked more questions when we started reading books about how I was going to be a Big Sister. I was on board with the Big part, but I didn't totally understand the Sister aspect. The Big Sister in the books seemed to be having a lot of fun with her baby doll, so that was cool. Yes, the entire family seemed a little too focused on the doll, but who was I to judge? Even baby dolls need love, I guess.

I wasn't quite sure the doll warranted its own entire room, but I stayed quiet when my parents started painting my old room a new color and brought in teddy bear décor to replace what I thought were perfectly acceptable pink safari animals. These two watch a lot of HGTV, so it wasn't out of the ordinary for them to completely overhaul a room for no apparent reason. Little did I know what was going to be in the "After" picture this time.

Sure, maybe I should have taken more notice of mom's growing belly, but anyone can tell you that mom's belly has a way of fluctuating in size even when a person hasn't crawled up into it (I'm still fuzzy on the exact details of the belly enlargement). In fact, I just assumed I was the reason her belly was getting so big. She's always blaming me for the fact that she doesn't look like her Throwback Thursday photos anymore, so maybe I did something to cause this change in appearance too.

And yes, the suspicious number of babies I was made to hold and pretend to find adorable in the last few months should have sent up warning signals. But if you had any idea how many times a day these people make me hold a prop or put me in a ridiculous outfit just so they can take a photo, you would understand that a little hysteria over how cute I looked holding a baby did not stand out as noteworthy.

I look cute doing everything, obviously.

Which is why I didn't bat an eye when mom set up that photo shoot. The woman enjoys a photoshoot. Yes, it seemed a bit out of character that she would want to take so many photos of her large belly, but I was proud of her for finally accepting that beauty comes in all shapes and sizes. Posing naked for a picture in a field while cradling that belly did seem like a little too much self-acceptance in my opinion, but hey, you do you, Mommy.

I feel like such a fool that I was worried about Mommy when Grandma said we were going to visit her in the hospital. I thought it must be pretty serious if both of my parents had stayed there overnight. But now I know that not only was mom okay, but the two of them had been *cheating* on me by having a sleepover with *another* child. As I said before—some bullshit.

Since we have been home, I've slowly started to accept that no one but me wants this new kid to leave. In fact, there seems to be a parade of people coming to the house to welcome the thing. I'm calling it a "thing" because it doesn't actually do anything that an actual person does.

People keep asking me if I'm excited to have a new friend to play with. These people are really underestimating my playing abilities, or perhaps they are unaware of the sort of head control that is needed to ride a scooter around the backyard with me. Either way, I feel like we could have just adopted a dog if the primary goal was to give me a playmate.

And we could have just put the dog in a crate at night, instead of the entire neighborhood needing to be awake while my playmate screams his face off for no reason. Dogs are notoriously great sleepers, you know.

Perhaps if I had been consulted at all about this addition to the family, I could have brought up some of these points that were clearly not given enough consideration.

That photographer is back today, the one who convinced mom to get naked in the field. Most people would consider that to be the type of person that shouldn't be allowed around children. But, in keeping with bad ideas, mom has invited this person into our home. At some point soon I'm going to have to get the authorities involved in this deteriorating situation I'm being made to live in.

This photographer, in addition to her questionable morals, clearly has no artistic eye. Which is a much greater sin, if you ask me. I look as cute as any kid has ever looked. My hair is bouncing with ringlets and has just the right number of bows. My outfit is on point, and even my shoes are off-the-charts adorable.

But who does this "photographer" want to take pictures of? The blob. Seriously! The blob isn't even awake, and this lady is putting ridiculous hats on its head and standing on chairs to get the best angle of it sleeping naked. I can't say I felt bad for her when the blob pooped all over that pretty blanket of hers. Even I know that the only thing this kid really knows how to do is soil things.

In a sign of what my life has now become, this hack is only interested in taking photos of me if the blob is also in the shot. Does she not remember how I rocked those pre-nudity field photos all by myself?

My parents look as if they haven't slept in a week (this is most likely because they haven't slept in a week) so I'll do them a solid and play along with this photoshoot. When the wall-size canvases of these photos are delivered, it will be clear to everyone who the real star is. (Hint: it's not the one pooping himself.)

And if that isn't enough to bring the spotlight back to me, I have one more trick up my sleeve. I'm not going to go into a lot of detail here, but suffice it to say my parents might want to start Googling the word "regression."

SOME PROFESSIONAL HELP

Introducing a new baby to the family can be a delicate process. This new child won't change how much you love your first child, but your firstborn may not see it that way.

I asked psychotherapist Gail Marie Poverman-Kave for some advice on how to ease kids into the idea of welcoming another child into their space. She recommended a lot of discussion leading up to the arrival: "Discuss names, what the baby will look like, whether it will be a boy or girl. You can have the older sibling help get the nursery ready."

When it comes to making a place for the new baby, you may need to move Child #1 out of their room or crib. Try not to make it too obvious that the older child is being kicked out because another kid is coming to take their place. That's the less-than-sensitive approach. Instead, trick your child into thinking the new Big Kid Bed and/or Big Kid Room is an exciting event that is in no way connected to all those tiny onesies that have been piling up.

Making the transition well in advance of the new baby's arrival will be in the best interest of both you and your child. A new bed or room can take some time to get used to, and you definitely don't want to be working out those kinks while also dealing with a newborn.

Poverman-Kave warns that the age of Child #1 can affect how he or she reacts to a new sibling: "Children of different ages will experience the baby's arrival differently. The older a child is, the more challenging it may be for them to share your attention. Children under two years old really won't understand the concept of having a new baby, whereas school-aged children may experience blatant jealousy. Making sure your older child has enough attention and is included in pictures and videos is very helpful toward alleviating their fears."

To help your older child feel involved and important when the new baby arrives, she suggests: "Allow the older child to participate in caring for the baby; bathing, singing, feeding, changing. Don't make this a chore or the child will resent the baby. Make it a time to bond with both children and encourage a healthy relationship between them."

Also, take time away from the new baby to shower Child #1 with attention. Give lots of hugs, head out for a quick fast food date with just the two of you, or offer praise for both the help he or she gives with the new baby and for things that have nothing to do with that annoying kid. These gestures don't need to be grand (you probably won't have the energy or time for grand), but even taking a few seconds to acknowledge your older child or give them a big hug will remind them that they are still important.

Making sure you are doing right by your new baby and your firstborn can be overwhelming. Most of the time, it can feel like you are giving both of them less than they deserve. Be forgiving of everyone in your household during this time of transition; you'll all get the hang of it eventually.

And no matter how hard it is now, never forget that someday you'll think to yourself, "Man, it was easier when only one of them was mobile." These, my friend, are the good old days.

Journal Entry
A LETTER TO VIVIAN

Dear Vivian,

In a little while you will move from being an Only Child to a Big Sister. How is that possible? You are still a baby in my eyes. I think you'll always be, to tell you the truth. No matter how big you get I will always think of you as my bean. We gave you that nickname when you were still in my belly, when we could barely see your tiny little beating heart on the ultrasound. My pregnancy books said you were only the size of a bean. We didn't know your gender, but we talked about you constantly, so a name was needed. "Bean" it was.

When you point at my belly these days, I tell you that there is a baby inside. I tell you that you were once a tiny baby in my belly too and that soon this baby will be out of my belly and in our house. You nod, but you don't have any idea what the hell I'm talking about.

I don't blame you. It doesn't make a lot of sense to me either, and it's happening in my belly. When I quiz you about the location of the baby, you instantly pull up your shirt and point to your own belly. Close enough, really.

I'm scared about bringing this new baby home. But not for the reasons I was scared to bring you home.

When I brought you home, I was just as new to this game as you were. I had a little more head control than you, but other than that we were both blank slates. That scared the crap out of me because the one thing I knew for sure was that nothing was more important than doing right by you. It didn't seem fair that you had been given a mom who had no idea what the hell she was doing.

But you didn't seem to mind. You nuzzled into the bend of my arm and snuggled your face against my breast as soon as you popped out. What you lacked in head control, you more than made up for in confidence that we were going to be okay. And what I lacked in confidence, I made up for in determination to prove you right.

So we headed off together, you and me. My beautiful little girl and a woman who never even liked babies before she met you. And together we figured it out. Eventually you even held up that head of yours. It was an exciting time indeed.

We had hiccups along the way, to be sure. You spent your first New Year's Eve repeatedly projectile vomiting all over both of us. I accidently let you roll off the couch a couple of times. I tried, and mostly failed, to figure out how to keep my clients happy and also be a good mom to you. And let's not forget about our difference of opinion regarding acceptable sleeping habits. It was rarely easy. But you never promised it would be easy. You only promised it would be worth it.

And, man, has it been worth it. Every second has been worth it as I've watched you grow more into a little person with each passing day. You are funny and kind, gentle yet brave. I see so

>

much of myself when I look at you, but it's even more exciting that every day I get a glimpse of the woman you are going to be.

We have a good thing going, our little family of three.

And that is why I'm scared this time.

What is going to happen when we bring home another kid? When you are no longer my one and only? Will he take up too much of my time, leaving you feeling abandoned? Will you know that I still want to hold you close, even though there is now another baby in my arms? Will you even remember the time when you were the only one, or will your childhood memories always play back with a cast of four?

I don't know exactly how things are going to go once your brother arrives. But one thing I know for sure—there will always be a place in my heart that is only yours. It's the place that holds those two years we had together, when we were both brand-new. I will never forget everything you taught me in those years about babies, about parenting, and about my own heart.

That heart, once closed off to so many of life's joys, was burst wide open the second I saw a positive symbol on my pregnancy test. From that moment on I have loved you with every ounce of my soul.

I loved feeling your endless flips when you were inside my belly; I loved how you burst into the world kicking and screaming. I love that once you were here, you always looked at me as if I were perfect, and you were quick to let it slide when it turned out I wasn't. Most of all, I love that no matter how big you get or what changes come our way, you will always be my bean. My sweet girl who fit perfectly into the bend of my arm. Just one of my many parts I've come to realize was made just for you.

2

BABY #1 WILL HAVE NO PATIENCE FOR YOUR PREGNANCY

Less nausea, more hustle, lady

OPTIONS FOR TRANSPORTING YOUR KIDS

DOUBLE STROLLER   "WEAR" THE BABY   "WEAR" BOTH KIDS

*E*VEN IF YOU had a rough first pregnancy, it tends to fade into the background as soon as your baby arrives. Your child's tiny button nose and easy giggles make any pregnancy struggles seem worth it. So much so that eventually you think embarking on another forty-week adventure sounds like a fantastic idea. (There is a good possibility that you are making poor decisions because you haven't slept since your first child arrived.)

But, mentally impaired or not, you forge on.

I know many women who enjoyed the process of making a human inside their body. My MOFL said things like, "I loved being pregnant!" and "I would totally do it again!" There is endless talk of all the "glowing" women do when they are gestating. I tell you about all of these things because there is a very good possibility you have had or will have a similar experience. And if you do, I don't want to hear about it.

For those of us with unpleasant pregnancy experiences, nothing inspires our rage quite like hearing tales of how others "loved" the process. We would come smack you for daring to utter the words, but we are pretty busy putting our head in a public toilet right now. We'll catch up with you later.

My first pregnancy started out with five months of all-day nausea and was generally an unpleasant experience. But even with that advance notice, I was still in a bit of denial when the excitement of pregnancy #2 gave way to the familiar nausea I hated so much.

I started stockpiling crackers and Tums. I hoped that maybe this time I wouldn't get hit so hard. Maybe a little ginger ale and some saltines would do the trick this go-around. Nothing to see here, people, just a woman keeping up with any and all of her responsibilities despite the fact that she is growing a placenta!

And if I were to compare my pregnancies, I would say my second was a bit easier. During Vivian's gestation I had to sit down and force myself to take bites of food. I would breathe in and out heavily, then chew, chew, chew, and swaaaaaallow against every vomiting urge my body was throwing at me. I lost ten pounds in my first trimester.

With Daniel I had the same twenty-four-hours-a-day "I'm going to puke" feeling, but I could calm it a bit if I just kept eating. I didn't quite shed the pounds with his pregnancy.

But what Daniel's pregnancy lacked in complete nausea misery, it made up for in unstoppable toddler energy.

This time I couldn't just climb into bed and pull my covers over my head for the entire day if I felt like crap. Because this time Vivian was sitting on the bed next to me bouncing. "Mommy, get up!"

So up I would get. And by "up" I mean "propped up" on the couch while letting the child watch as much TV as is allowable by law (sorry about your brain cells, Vivi, mommy was growing a placenta).

Vivian was not a fan of Mommy's new couch affinity and because she was only eighteen months old, she could not comprehend why I was suddenly no fun whatsoever. I told her that her baby sister or brother was inside my belly and that was why I was so tired, but she had no time for such explanations. "Less excuses, more chasing me around in a circle for twenty minutes, lady."

I did my best to keep up with her, but most days I couldn't muster up the energy for anything other than saying, "Instead of hide and go seek, let's play a game where mommy lies on the floor and you bury her in pillows!"

It was actually a hard time in my relationship with my daughter; I think she felt abandoned by the mom she had gotten used to. For the duration of my pregnancy I wasn't much fun, I had very little patience, and I was exhausted. All. The. Time. Also, in a weird way, as my belly got bigger and bigger, her sibling was literally pushing her farther and farther off my lap. She pulled away from me and grabbed on to Becky during my pregnancy, and it absolutely broke my heart. (I had a few hormones helping out in that area.)

I remember during particularly dark times I would be battling Vivian, who was screaming, "I no like Mommy!" while also battling the unborn child, who was sending waves of nausea through my body. I would think to myself, "I'm going through all of this pregnancy crap and I'm just going to give birth to a kid who hates me!" (I'm not sure I can overstate how many hormones were involved in my general thought process.)

After Daniel arrived it was so much fun to finally be able to pick Vivian up and throw her around. She didn't know what to make of it at first because it had been so long since I was able to be physical with her. I played with her as long as she wanted and made a point of not being the one to stop the fun because I was tired or out of breath.

Slowly but surely, Vivi and I reconnected, and both of us enjoyed having me back in an unpregnant state. Although our idea of normal had changed a bit to include a newborn, no sleep, and our house in complete disorder, I think both Vivian and I felt a shift in our relationship when at least my body started to get back to something close to what she used to know. My energy levels increased, I was physically able to do so many more things, and I could now focus solely on her for extended periods of time while Becky watched the baby. She got her mommy back, and she was quick to welcome me. Although her mommy still favored any game that could involve lying on the floor because obviously.

Moms on the Front Lines

PREGNANCY, THE SEQUEL

As I mentioned previously, most of my MOFL just loooooved being pregnant. Their tales of peaceful gestation have no place among my complaining, so I reached out to the moms who had less than harmonious experiences.

Jen, mom of two, had to get creative when she was put on partial bed rest with pregnancy #2: "My cervix was super soft. So basically I had to lie on the couch and learn how to parent Child #1 (eighteen months old) horizontally. The best way to keep him entertained was to have him drive his little cars all over my body or to eat ice cream together (that one made me feel better as well). I carried Baby #2 all the way to term. Needless to say she slid *riiiiiiight* out!"

Carrie had some physical issues as well: "I had some pretty intense pelvis bone issues. Basically they didn't 'relax' together. I just bore it with #1, but with #2 they put me on a no-stairs, no-incline, and no-running restriction. They basically said, 'Don't move unless you have to,' which was okay by me because I couldn't muster the courage to anyway. Trying to chase a toddler was awesome. I had *lots* of visits to the chiropractor to make the pregnancy even remotely tolerable."

I really wanted to hear from **Debbie**, mom of five, because I knew that she was sick for the entirety of *all* of her pregnancies. That's 200 weeks of puking she's endured in her lifetime. The woman deserves a medal of honor, in my opinion.

I asked Debbie how she survived her awful pregnancies when there were other kids around who needed to be tended to: "You just have to deal with it and get creative. Some days I would have Grace sit on the bathroom floor with me while I threw up and we would read stories between hurls. 'Let's read *Biscuit*!'. . . BLECH . . . 'Oh, what's he doing now? That silly dog.'"

One thing Debbie did differently than me was to just embrace the pukage. I spent my days fighting my nausea, so afraid that if I started puking I would have to be put on medication because I wasn't retaining enough nutrients. Debbie had a much more efficient plan: "I learned not to fight the feeling. It was easier if I just tried to get it out of my system when I felt it coming on. If I tried to hold it in and function, it was far worse when it finally did come out."

"So I would excuse myself to the restroom regardless of where I was. I was in and out in a few minutes. The kids knew the most because, of course, they follow you to the bathroom. Sometimes you would see their little sweet sides come out and they would sit and pat me on the back and tell me it's going to be okay. It was a nice bonding time for us, oddly."

When I asked Debbie how she was able to keep eating through her sickness, she shared this wonderful technique: "You kind of learn what foods get you through. I would eat a couple bites of a green apple, knowing that it would make me puke faster, and then I would eat a full meal after. The shit we do!"

You just know your day is going to be solid when your To Do List starts with (1) Eat apple, (2) Puke up apple and everything else in stomach, (3) Eat breakfast, and (4) Repeat for all other meals. Ahhhhh, pregnancy is just a *miracle,* isn't it?!

If your particular miracle isn't as easy as you'd hoped, try to give yourself a little wiggle room on acceptable parenting practices for a few months. Load up the DVR with Pixar movies and bribe the child with engaging toys if they will buy you a few minutes of quiet. Don't worry, their IQ will bounce right back after your pregnancy.

Also, don't be afraid to ask for help. Let your partner know that they are going to need to step up their game a bit while you face-plant on the couch. Or ask a friend to babysit for a couple of hours while you lie facedown somewhere else.

And if anyone questions you, just tell them, "I'm building a placenta over here! Leave me alone!" Don't worry, your scowl will have a beautiful pregnancy glow, so no one will be offended.

Journal Entry

A TALE OF TWO PREGNANCIES

Pregnancy #1

Average Doctor's Visit: 1 hour

Doctor: "Okay, so everything looks good, do you guys have any questions?"

Becky and I look at each other. Where to start, really?

Me: "How long will I feel like shit?"

Becky: "Is there anything I should be doing?"

Me: "Can you check the heartbeat again? I'm worried."

"Can I take Tums?"

"How much weight should I be gaining?"

"Can I sleep on my back?"

"Which side should I sleep on? I read that I can hurt the baby if I sleep on the wrong side."

"How big is the baby? Is that how big it is supposed to be?"

"How many different birthing/parenting/breastfeeding classes do you guys offer? Can I take them more than once?"

"Should I be walking more? Will that help with the delivery?"

"What is the pain I have right here? And right here? Does that mean the baby is in danger?"

"There are some really scary things I read on the Internet that I want to discuss."

"Is there something we can use at home to monitor the baby? To make sure it is okay?"

"When is the soonest we can find out the gender?"

"What is the longest delivery you've ever seen?"

"Is there a form I can fill out right now for my epidural?"

"Do you have more informational pamphlets I can take home?"

"What books do you recommend?"

"When did your kids start sleeping through the night?"

"Will I start liking babies once I have mine?"

Becky: "We ordered the nursery furniture. Do you think it will get here before the baby?"

Pregnancy #2

Average Doctor's Visit: 10 minutes (including the time it takes to find a parking spot)

Doctor: "Okay, we weighed and measured you. Everything looks good. Any questions?"

Me: "Those little gas bubbles I'm feeling are actually the baby moving, right? I didn't know that last time."

Doctor: "Yep."

Me: "Cool."

Doctor: "Anything else? Any issues?"

Me: "I feel like shit all the time and I can't stand the smell of garlic."

Doctor: "Yeah, that'll happen."

Me: "All right! See you next time!"

Doctor: "Tell Becky I said hello."

Me: "Will do!"

3 IT'S TIME TO GET ANOTHER WATERMELON OUT OF YOU

D-day, take two

A TALE OF TWO BIRTHS

FIRST BIRTH

SECOND BIRTH

S O HERE WE go again. Another D-day coming your way.

The good news is that you are just about done rocking the "eighteen months pregnant" look you've had for the last three months of your gestation. The bad news is that you are about to start rocking the "Oh, she has two kids" look. That style is a little more long term. Spoiler alert.

If you've read my first book, you know that my first birth was *looney tunes*. If you didn't read that book, then I'll give you a brief summary: Dawn doesn't want to get to the hospital too early, so she labors a little too long at home. By the time Dawn arrives at the hospital, she is screaming her face off and wants all the drugs. The nurses think she's a wimp but upon further inspection realize that she's actually nine and a half centimeters dilated. She is still screaming for all the drugs. She doesn't get any of the drugs. Forty-five minutes later the baby pops out. The End.

Looney tunes.

The first time around, my birth plan read in its entirety: "Drugs. All the drugs. Then find some more drugs and give those to me as well, thank you." What I ended up with was no drugs, and a sliced hoo-ha. So things went a bit off-script.

For my second birth, I assumed things would go down roughly the same. I've heard over and over that babies come faster with each birth, so I was half expecting to deliver the boy in my bathroom at home.

Even though my first birthing experience was insane (and I went a little insane during the experience), I was less scared the second time around. Part of the terror of childbirth is the unfortunate math you face (one watermelon needing to get out through a-less-than-watermelon-size hole as its most popular escape method), along with having no idea how that math is going to play out.

During my first pregnancy, I said repeatedly (at least once a day) that my biggest fear (beyond something bad happening to the baby) was getting to the hospital too late for drugs. Then, oopsie, I got to the hospital too late for drugs. My biggest fear came true and I made it through (with the help of quite a few expletives).

So although I wasn't looking forward to a replay of the first delivery, I also wasn't terrified of a replay. I had survived it before and could do it again. I even went so far as to proclaim that I was going to try to go drug-free again, since I knew I could do it. I'm woman, hear me roar (through the slicing of a hoo-ha)!

Vivian was one week early and came so fast that I was scared to venture too far from home in the month leading up to Daniel's arrival. At any moment I could go into labor! And then if the labor was anything like my first, I might barely have time to get to the hospital! Everyone stay on high alert!!

But then Daniel's due date came and went without incident. He was kicking and twirling and assaulting my ribs and bladder with abandon, in no hurry to make his appearance.

At a week overdue I had to go in for an appointment, presumably to see if I was going for the world's longest pregnancy. It was the middle of a squelching-hot summer, I felt like I weighed 400 pounds, and I was more than a little dramatic.

When I got to the doctor's office, they hooked me up to a monitor to see how things were going with my lazy child. Everything seemed fine until Daniel's heartbeat dipped a bit. It went right back up, but that dip ensured I wasn't leaving the hospital anytime soon.

My mom rushed over to the hospital because the last time she barely made it before the baby popped out. We arranged to have someone watch Vivian. And then we waited. And monitored. And waited some more. I was having a few contractions, but they were so mild I wouldn't put them on the scale much higher than mild gas pains. Daniel was still in no hurry.

After quite a few hours of waiting, the doctors recommended putting me on Pitocin to move things along a bit. I really didn't want to do Pitocin because I'd heard bad things about the contractions you get as a result of taking it. And I also really didn't want to put random drugs into my body just because the boy was in no rush to exit. But the doctors didn't like that Daniel's heart had dipped even once, so they really wanted to get him moving toward an exit. I held out for a while as several doctors and nurses came to make their pro-Pitocin pitches. Eventually, they convinced me that it was in the baby's best interest to help him along. The contractions did come on stronger, but I was okay. I was woman, hear me—wait, those contractions were starting to feel pretty serious. Last time I felt contractions like that I was holding a baby an hour later. So things were probably going to start moving quickly now. Here we go!

I asked the nurse to check me because I was pretty sure I was about to have a baby.

She checked me and I was five centimeters dilated. Which means I wasn't anywhere near having a baby.

So that's when I decided that I needed all the drugs. Because I am woman, hear me medicate.

After I got the drugs, things slowed down again, which is what usually happens when you get the drugs. We all waited. And waited.

The nurses at our hospital were on eight-hour shifts. We were there long enough for the first nurse we had to come back to work. She was very excited to be back for the birth. So excited that even though it was about time to start pushing, she asked if I could wait until she got back from her break to deliver the boy. I said sure.

This is hilarious because it is so far removed from the crazy that was my first delivery.

FIRST DELIVERY

Nurse: *"Don't push just yet; we aren't ready."*

Me: *"I'm pushing; she's ready!"*

SECOND DELIVERY

Nurse: *"I'll be right back. Hold on a few minutes and we'll start pushing."*

Me: *"No rush. I can't feel a thing; take your time!"*

My first birth was marked by screaming and my mind breaking from the intensity, but my second birth was strangely calm, even though I was still pushing a watermelon out of me. This time I was using my phone to take pictures of the doctor between pushes; the first time I was repeatedly crying, "I can't do this" between pushes.

Before Vivian was born, the doctors weren't able to monitor her successfully, so there were roughly fourteen thousand medical people in the room awaiting her arrival. (She was fine, but I was a bit mortified at the number of people staring at my lady bits.) Daniel was well monitored for hours, so our delivery room was decidedly less occupied and chaotic. The only medical personnel this time were our excited nurse and our doctor, who was the calmest little man you've ever seen. He watched the monitor intensely, cued me to push, and when Daniel unexpectedly came out with the cord wrapped around his neck twice the doctor slowly and precisely removed it without comment.

The only stress of Daniel's birth came when he popped out and wasn't breathing. They took him away from me and worked on him for what felt like an hour. (I think it was a couple of minutes.) Eventually his little cry filled the room, and all was well with the world.

That little bit of stress actually marked the biggest difference between my two births. When I was handed Vivian for the first time I was still in shock from the whirlwind of her delivery. I held her tight and told her I loved her, but I didn't actually have any maternal emotions going through my body. Mostly I just had residual adrenaline pumping. As I wrote in my first *Sh!t* book, it took me weeks to feel bonded with my first baby.

When Daniel came out and needed help right away, I immediately forgot about his birth and started worrying about his health. While the nurse was trying to get him to take his first breath, I was holding mine. Then, when I finally heard his little cry, I wanted nothing more than to grab him up in my arms and hold him tight. My mommy instincts kicked in immediately.

I had been afraid that Daniel would be delivered early, possibly in my bathroom, because he would come out so quickly. He was a week late and took a full day to arrive. I thought I would have a natural birth again, and instead I got all the drugs. I was worried that I wouldn't quite know what to do with my newborn when he arrived, but we hit it off right away.

That second childbirth was a great introduction to how things would generally go with my second child. And that's to say things never quite went the way I was expecting them to go. In some ways, it was a scary thing (cord wrapped around his neck), and in others it was lovely (drugs/bonding/drugs).

I grabbed him up as soon as I could and whispered, "Hi." Over and over again into his brand-new ears. And so began my Daniel Adventure.

Moms on the Front Lines

SO MANY CHILDBIRTHS

My MOFL group is very handy because they've had their share of experiences with children. Never is this more apparent than when you ask them to detail their childbirths. Good lord, do these women have a lot of birthing experience under their belts (literally).

Some of my moms have had two, and even three, births that were very similar. Some, like **Kaysee**, birther of three, even went so far as to proclaim that her births were enjoyable. Clearly, there is something wrong with Kaysee: "I love the process of giving birth! I would like to have another baby just for that part. The

>

contractions, the pain, and the exhilaration and joy of seeing your baby for the first time is so amazing to me! It is all so worth it!" I'm going to assume Kaysee had three epidurals.

Dana, mom of two, loved her drugs: "Based on my experiences, I would give birth over getting a bikini wax any day of the week! I did have epidurals with both and they were awesome! Overall, I loved the whole experience!"

These women are throwing around a lot of exclamation points in their descriptions of childbirth. Exclamation points that don't follow cuss words. That confuses me.

Debbie, who gave birth *five* times, said that every one of her deliveries was different: "I've done it almost every way. I had an emergency C-section after hours of labor; a totally natural and drug-free birth; an epidural that almost ended in an emergency C-section because the kid was so late and didn't want to come out; and lastly I tapped out and planned a C-section as soon as humanly possible."

I need some meds just reading about Debbie's experiences.

On the no-drug front, Michelle had her two boys with no help from an epidural. Both boys came quickly, but her first birth was much more traumatic: "I had severe hemorrhaging, passed out, and required a blood transfusion. It was an awful experience. It took me three weeks before I was able to walk farther than the bathroom. My second labor was a breeze.

"I was stubborn and said I wasn't going to have an epidural no matter what, since I'd done it before and I knew I could do it again. I was dilated to a six when I arrived at the hospital, but didn't have severely painful contractions until my water broke forty minutes before I delivered. Two pushes and my son was out. Recovery was much smoother and breastfeeding was so much easier since my body wasn't in shock."

I love the badasses who can stick with their no-drug birth plans (I'm not so badass in this area).

Sarah G. has given birth to four kids by a variety of delivery methods: "My first was crazy. Even working in the gyn world now, I know it was crazy. But we got it done vaginally, with a laundry list of interventions! Number three was an amazing VBAC. Number four was an awesome labor. I just rolled with it. It hurt but it was okay. When it was time to push I may or may not have freaked out, crossed my legs, crawled up the bed, and almost kicked my doctor in the face, all while screaming, 'I can't do it; just pull it out of me!' And so he did."

Sarah G.'s second delivery was the hardest on her emotionally: "Number two was an unplanned C-section. For me, the C-section was a definite difference. It was super-easy compared to my first delivery, but I hated the experience. It took me longer to bond with number two. I have always felt like my vaginal births were bonding, like we went through something together and worked hard together. After my vaginal births, I got to hold my baby right away (even if briefly). With my second baby I remember kissing his head, and the next thing I recall they were waking me up because he wanted to eat. My friends and family had all held him and met him before me. It really broke my heart that all these people knew my baby before me. It made me sad that he waited an hour or longer to eat after he arrived. I hated the experience and still do!"

Sarah G.'s story is a good reminder about how much your child's birth can affect your initial bonding. Keep this in mind when you head out for your next delivery and know that it's totally normal if you don't immediately bond with your newborn. You aren't broken, and neither is the baby. Sometimes things take a little bit longer to snap into place.

Michaela, mom of two, had a scary birth experience with her first child. She was at the hospital for blood work because her son was overdue. She was on a monitor while waiting for her blood results and the baby's heartbeat disappeared (or at least sounded like it did). She was rushed into an emergency C-section and was told afterward that they only had about seven minutes to act before his lowered heart rate would have been damaging or fatal to the baby. Needless to say, she has always felt so incredibly lucky that she happened to be hooked up to a monitor when the baby's heart rate dipped. I asked her if that experience left her scared for delivery #2.

"After what happened with Sam, I knew anything was possible. A sudden loss, yes, but also the universe intervening and making good, miraculous stuff happen too. So, I didn't worry the second time around like you'd think I might have. I was just hoping really hard for the best possible outcome. All that said, when I actually went into 'labor' (I wasn't dilating, so maybe it wasn't officially labor) and I was in triage with the heart monitor, they said I would have to leave since I wasn't dilated. I felt really strongly in that moment that I or the baby would die if we left. I actually said, 'I'll die!'

"Also, the heart monitor kept slipping off my belly and the room would go quiet like it did when Sam's heart rate cut out and it was just too much. That's when I got a little scared. When the midwife came back and said, 'C-section?' it was easy to say yes to get to point B (safe, healthy, delivered baby) as fast as possible. Maybe if I hadn't had the experience we had with Sam, I would have worked through that moment, but . . . who knows."

Your second birth may turn out to be exactly like your first, and that may be a comforting or terrifying thought. Or it may be a completely different journey to the finish line. There is no telling how your next delivery will play out, but this would be as good a time as any to let go of any expectations you have for Baby #2, for birth and beyond. Little Dos is second to the party, but he or she will bring so many unexpectedly awesome new things with them.

And if you're lucky like me, the first awesome thing they bring will be drugs. What better way to start a new relationship, really?

BREASTFEEDING IS STILL F'N HARD
Your poor boobs have been through a lot

MULTI-TASKING

- - - - - - - - - - - - - - - - - - - -

The Bad News is that my boobs are ridiculously saggy from breastfeeding multiple children.

The Good News is that I can breastfeed the baby on the floor while I cook dinner.

*I*F YOU ARE to believe the Internet, baby books, and every judgmental mom out there, breastfeeding is the most natural thing on the planet. It's what our bodies were made to do, really. If you want your child to be a healthy, smart, functioning member of society you will breastfeed them with abandon. Nature demands it!

But then, nature isn't always easy to work with. All we want to do is feed our baby with our boobs, and nature decides to throw in lovely hurdles such as mastitis, latching challenges, low milk production, and bloody nipples. Really, nature?!

When you venture into feeding Baby #2, you will be presented with a unique new hurdle: your firstborn.

Even if you struggled with breastfeeding your first baby, it was probably a relatively quiet undertaking. You'd snuggle up on a couch or a rocking chair. Once you got into the breastfeeding groove, you may have even kicked up your feet and read a book on your Kindle while the child peacefully ate at your bosom. It was a scene that would be accompanied by a sweet lullaby if it were part of a movie.

You should probably go ahead and erase that scene from your mind as you prepare to breastfeed Baby #2. Because the soundtrack to your upcoming adventure is going to be decidedly less angelic.

This time there will be no quietly slipping away to the nursery to feed the baby on the blue or pink rocking chair that is tucked in the corner. Because nothing happens quietly once you have multiple children in the house (see Chapter 12: "Everything Is So Damn Loud"). Quiet has left the building.

This time your newborn will have to develop a steel grip from day one in order to hang on to your boob during feedings because this ride will be a bumpy one. You'll try your best to nurse the second child while in a leisurely sitting position on the couch, but your firstborn will instantly begin to dismantle your entire home as soon as your butt hits a cushion. You'll be up and down, moving from left to right. You'll be trying to grab Child #1 with your arms or your legs as he or she wizzes past you defiantly.

Instead of snoozing while enjoying a light afternoon snack, the baby will have to develop a tolerance for mom's random outbursts during mealtime. "Stop!" "Don't you throw that!" "You better go pick that up, or you're going to be in trouble." "I'll get up, I will! Don't make me get up!" "Don't you run away from me!"

BABY #1

Enya playing over a scene of tranquility and maternal bliss (with the occasional bloody nipple thrown in).

BABY #2

Black Sabbath playing over a scene of a baby flopping off your boob while you chase a toddler around the living room. (Your nipples may not even be on your body at this point.)

Even more fun than all of this is attempting to pump while corralling the two children. You'll get yourself all hooked up to the contraption, in full dairy cow mode, and then you'll be left to parent with only your feet. The children will sense that there is a cord attaching you to the wall, and that will set off the misbehave sensor in their brains. Even the innocent baby will find a way to wreak havoc (think rolling around in his own spit-up during tummy time).

And there you will be, reaching as far as possible with your arms and legs while trying not to move too much because your nipples are attached to machinery. You'll actually surprise yourself with how much you can accomplish when you are able to use only your toes. But I'm not sure this was the image you had when you were bouncing up and down celebrating your positive pregnancy test for Baby #2.

You may actually start to look forward to late-night feedings, as the middle of the night brings along with it a calming peace. Try not to focus too much on the fact that it's only peacefully quiet because everyone else on the planet is sound asleep. That might diminish the calm a bit. Just treasure these few feedings that aren't interrupted by the antics or demands of Child #1. Maybe even read a couple pages of your Kindle book, if you can manage to keep your eyes open. Or better yet, close those eyes and celebrate the fact that there is no reason you need to be on high alert.

If you have your children close enough together, then you will also experience the joy that is breastfeeding one child while potty training the other. Nothing really brings home the reality of having two kids quite like this unique combo of parental responsibilities.

You turn on the TV, put extra toys on the floor, and organize your phone, the remote, and a potential bribing snack for Child #1 on the couch next to you. Everything is in place for a successful nursing session. You settle in with the baby for a feeding. Things are going smoothly, the older child is playing contently, and the TV seems to be doing its intended job of sucking the brain matter out of Child #1's head. All is calm, all is bright.

And then.

"Mommy, I have to go poop."

You've just started potty training so asking, "Can you hold it for a few minutes?" is not an option. The only two options are to take the child to the bathroom while the baby hangs from your boob or let the child crap their pants (and possibly your floor). Depending on how exhausted you are, you may actually consider both options to be viable.

If you are going with option 1, you have to move quickly because at this early stage of potty training the announcement of the poop and the arrival of the poop happen very close together. The baby holds on for dear life as you run down the hallway (shirtless) toward the bathroom with the poop-in-progress child. You get into the bathroom and bend down to help the child take off her pants and get on the toilet.

There is a 50 percent chance she won't actually make it to the toilet before pooping, and a 100 percent chance that you will be wiping a butt with one hand while holding a baby to your boob with the other hand. You are like a Cirque du Soleil acrobat with your balancing abilities, really. And the three of you have just put on quite a show.

As fun as this show sounds, you really haven't lived until this drill plays out in a public place. You just can't beat the excitement of a toddler announcing, "I have to poop!" in the middle of a restaurant while you are trying to discreetly nurse a baby. Next thing you know, you are running through the restaurant with your nursing cover barely covering anything, your baby randomly biting down on your nipple in an effort to hang on, and you pushing your child toward the public bathroom to do his business. Once you're in the bathroom, the germs on every surface start to call out to you, mocking you for thinking you will be able to keep either child from being doused in disease and filth during your time in here.

It will become very important for you to completely shut down all logical thoughts in your brain once you enter the bathroom stall. Because overthinking this situation is not going to do anyone any favors. Don't think about what has happened in this stall before you arrived. Don't think about your boobs flopping about in the wind. Don't think about how you are going to get the child's pants down and butt on or near the toilet while using only one hand. Definitely don't think about how you are going to wipe that butt while holding the baby and trying to keep your nursing cover out of the toilet.

Just move forward with each step. Keep a smile on your face, and don't let any of the screaming that is happening in your brain actually make its way out of your mouth. This bathroom will not break you. In fact, you are building up fantastic immunities during your time in this stall. (But just for fun, go ahead and drench all three of you in hand sanitizer as soon as you escape.)

It is at this point in your parenting life that you will start to understand why some women just adopt a bunch of cats and call it a day. Cats seem nice. And they are potty trained from birth. I think we can all agree that you should have given that option more consideration, really.

Moms on the Front Lines

BOOBS FOR CHILD #2

Breastfeeding, even at its best, is still a very difficult task to master. And it's rarely at its best.

My MOFL had varying degrees of success with their attempts to breastfeed their second child. Some struggled with getting their milk to come in at all, and others breastfed until the children were two years old. We have a range of boobs among us, really.

Jen was very traumatized by her first few months with two kids: "My first kid is crazy! I think I've mentally blocked out all memory of the time when I had a two-year-old and a newborn. Those were dark days. I know I had to use the TV even though I'm not huge on screen time. I also remember always having toys readily available in every room to keep the toddler entertained while I nursed. I pretty much had a preschool-type area set up in my living room for months."

Amy's experience was a little less harrowing: "It was incredibly entertaining, having a three-year-old watching my every move. And she often mimicked me by holding her baby doll against her chest, under her shirt. (So cute.)"

I remember Vivian did this as well, although she seemed to do it most often when we were out in public. It wasn't quite as cute when the waiter walked up to our table to find the two-year-old with her shirt up and a baby doll on her boob, declaring, "The baby is eating!"

Carrie's second son was a pro at nursing from day one, but he was also boob-exclusive: "He was fast and efficient and was done in like ten minutes tops. I didn't pump much the second time as #2 loved boob and only boob. Needless to say, we tried *every* bottle/nipple combo, but no go, boob was the only acceptable answer."

Deanna found it more difficult to breastfeed her second child: "He took *forever* to eat, and I never felt like I produced enough for him. It helped that my three-year-old was independent and loved to just sit and play. I also kept a special box of toys that she only played with when Daddy wasn't home and I was breastfeeding."

If you are insane like **Kaysee** and you plan your kids ridiculously close together, you might find that your lap becomes a very popular place: "My kids are fifteen-and-a-half months apart! It was a little challenging to nurse while also cuddling a one-year-old. My kids were not the best at nursing to begin with, and I did not always produce enough milk. So I only nursed my second child for about two months, and then I just pumped. This was partly because it was easier for my husband to help out with nighttime feedings and also because it was hard to sit down long enough to feed the baby when I still had to attend to a one-year-old. I have pictures of all three of us asleep on the loveseat. I would have my son sit next to me while I fed the baby and then they would both fall asleep. I didn't want to get up and wake one of them up, so the best alternative was for all of us to nap together!"

That was a great move on Kaysee's part. Because anytime both children are sleeping, it is recommended by all professionals (of the mental health variety) to do everything in your power to keep them in that state. It doesn't matter if your various body parts are going numb or you have to pee—you must not move until those children wake up. If I teach you only one thing, let this be it.

Michelle wanted to stay active with two kids, so she had to develop her nursing-on-the-go skills: "The big issue was learning to be comfortable nursing anywhere, anytime, since I didn't want to be stuck in the house all the time and Paxton was a frequent nurser. I nursed several times during mommy and me classes without a cover."

That f-it mentality is par for the second baby course. While the Internet and social media go crazy over whether a mom should cover up while nursing in public, tired moms just do whatever is easiest to get through the day, interwebs be damned. (See Chapter 8: "You May Be All Out of Shits" for more on this attitude shift.) Try to use this laid-back attitude to your advantage when dealing with all the joys that breastfeeding will throw your way.

Expect that it will be difficult in the beginning (and possibly in the middle and at the end as well). Lean heavily on television, iPads, and prohibited snacks to keep your first child in line during nursing sessions (nothing like polluting one kid while enriching the other). And pat yourself on the back for the amazing amount of things you are able to accomplish using one hand and a few toes. Motherhood rocks.

Journal Entry

DANIEL IS A BOOB MAN

I spent much of my daughter's early days trying to figure out how the hell to take care of a baby. A big part of that effort included trying to figure out how to feed her. Was she getting enough milk? Was she latched on correctly? How often should I be feeding her? Should I be supplementing with formula? Was it possible that she was actually sucking my nipples right off of my body? It was a confusing time, to say the least.

But sweet Daniel seemed to pop out of the womb looking for a boob. He was ecstatic when he found two for the taking. He was all in from the very beginning with breastfeeding. He latched on to them and didn't let go.

That was great because it meant we didn't have the weight-loss issues we'd had the first couple of days with Vivian. Daniel had no interest in losing weight; he was eating like an actor bulking up for a role. Unfortunately for my nipples, Daniel decided that eating every hour or so for the first few days was the only acceptable way to pack on the pounds.

My nipples, in shock from being thrown back into this abusive lifestyle, were absolutely raw at the beginning of their time with my second child. I tried a nipple shield and Daniel responded with a firm "No, thank you" to that solution. I spent most of my days shirtless, because anything rubbing up against the open wounds that I called breasts was excruciating. Showering felt like someone was throwing boiling water on my chest. Sleeping was only possible if I didn't move at all. I regularly saw blood mixed in with my pumped breast milk, which was more than a little alarming.

The only things that helped a little were nipple guards, rounded cones that I could wear over my nipples when I wasn't nursing. They kept my bra and shirt and any other foreign bodies from touching my skin and even had air holes to keep things ventilated. The cones weren't pointy, but they did extend my boobs an inch or so. Adding this padding to my already huge breastfeeding boobs left me looking officially stacked. So at least I had that going for me.

During this time we constantly tried to convince Daniel that a bottle of pumped breast milk would give him just as much satisfaction as my boobs. Not only did he disagree with that idea, but he was quite frankly offended by it. He would recoil from any synthetic nipple that was offered and demand, "Bring me my boobs!"

That battle cry became the general theme of Daniel's first year. He was Boob or Bust for the first eight months of his life. And what an exciting time that was for me.

Throughout his first eight months my boobs, and my body, were on Daniel's schedule. Every three hours during the day, and usually once or twice at night, my boobs needed to be available for the boy. Every day. And the boy enjoyed taking a good forty-five minutes on the boob. So that left me with about two hours to get anything done before I had to be back for a feeding. It wasn't the most flexible time.

Every once in a while, we would try to introduce a bottle, and every once in a while he would react as if we were offering him a

>

cigarette. And also as if we were burning him with the cigarette. He refused to take the bottle and instead decided that shrieking at the top of his lungs was an appropriate response to being offered sustenance.

I work from home, so on days when the kids had a sitter, she would just bring Daniel to me every three hours and I would put him on my lap to feed him while I worked. It was super-ergonomic.

About seven months after Daniel was born, I called a lactation specialist, pleading with her to find a way to get Daniel to accept something besides my boobs. She recommended I give up on the bottle and go straight to a sippy cup because Daniel might find that more entertaining. She also recommended that I be grateful for having this problem, because most of the people she worked with would give anything to have a baby who loves boobs. Humph. I guess she had a point, even though my nipples refused to embrace gratitude.

Around month eight, we introduced the sippy cup and solid foods, and Daniel was able to slowly recover from his boob addiction. Over time I reduced the number of feedings, although at each one he grabbed on to my breasts like one of the dogs you've seen in those YouTube videos who are so damn excited to welcome their soldier home from war: "I didn't think I'd ever see you again, sweet boobs! It's been a trying twelve hours!"

And then, after thirteen months, Daniel had to say goodbye to his boobs forever. They had a hell of a run together.

If I were being honest, I'd tell you that it wasn't all bad. In fact, it had a lot of really cool aspects. I had intended to cut him off on his first birthday, but it took me another month to give up that special time with my boy. Several times a day he would snuggle in close and rest on me while he ate. He took his time with eating, so the snuggles lasted a while. They were the best part of my days, those quiet times with my last baby.

So often the second kid seems to get thrown on a train that is already moving, and in a lot of ways Daniel had to try to keep up with everything going on around him from day one. We were a family (and most notably, a toddler) in motion, so there wasn't much time for Daniel to just be a baby.

But when he breastfed, everything slowed down. Daniel and I were in our own little space, and for a few minutes our train hit the brakes. I'm so incredibly lucky to have had those moments when he was brand-new. I often find myself missing that time with Daniel, especially now that he's moving faster than any train we've ever been on.

My raw nipples were a small price to pay for great bonding time with my boy, really. And on the upside, after two rounds of breastfeeding, my boobs are now so stretched out that I can twirl them around the way a flapper twirls her fringe. So at least I have that going for me.

YOU'RE A BIG BROTHER
(AND MOMMY IS A MESS!)

*B*RINGING A NEW baby home is met with general celebration and congratulations. Balloons are delivered, presents are wrapped, and all cards have happy messages on them.

I've always thought that those cards were not quite hitting the right tone for presentation to a woman who has just brought a new baby home. She is a ball of hormones, sleep deprivation, and poor hygiene. And then she is forced to move through what can be very dark days surrounded by mass quantities of gifts and quotes that are basically mocking her lack of appropriate joy.

I would like to start a line of cards that are a little more realistic. They would say things like, "You are not a bad mom if you are crying more than the baby." Or, "It's okay if you aren't as happy as the moms on the Johnson & Johnson commercials." But mostly, "You are not going crazy, you are not a failure, you don't need to hide."

Although postpartum sadness might not come as a total shock with your second baby, it can still take your legs out from underneath you when it hits. And unlike your first go-round, you now have a confused audience for your dark days. Trying to explain why mommy is crying might not go a long way in convincing Child #1 that this baby is a welcome addition to the family.

Postpartum sadness can range from a case of the "baby blues" to full-on postpartum depression and even postpartum psychosis. Talking to a doctor is the best way to figure out where you land on the scale, and it's also the best way to make sure you are getting whatever help you need. You are not going crazy, you are not a failure, you don't need to hide.

When I reached out to my MOFL about their experiences with postpartum issues, they said things like: "I didn't have postpartum depression, but I definitely rode the wave of hormones for a few months." One mom didn't get the emotions she was expecting: "Instead of feeling super emotional, I felt angry. There was a lot of rage." Another mom said, "I was never diagnosed with postpartum depression, but I sure was sad."

"I sure was sad" is where a lot of us land on the postpartum scale. We are functioning, we are doing the things moms are supposed to do, and we appear to have it together. But beneath that we are sad for no apparent reason. Like my moms above, maybe we don't even recognize that we are suffering from varying degrees of postpartum sadness.

Sarah G., mom of four, described her postpartum depression perfectly: "Everything felt like a chore. It was a time when everything should be joyful, but life just felt *really* hard. Getting dressed was hard. Leaving the house, touching base with friends, going to church—everything was so hard. I basically functioned at a bare minimum and slept."

Postpartum depression and baby blues are talked about a lot, but mostly in terms of other people having them. Maybe there is a little whisper about a mom friend who is suffering, or there is a story posted on social media about a woman who has done something terrible as a result of postpartum depression. But very rarely do you hear from the actual women who are going through it, at least not *when* they are going through it. Why is that? Why do we feel so ashamed of something that is heavily documented to be totally normal and expected following childbirth?

Before I had kids I would read stories of women who did horrible things to their kids while suffering from postpartum depression. I would shake my head at how awful the stories were and how awful the moms were. These days when I read those stories I feel so bad for everyone involved, including the mom.

She was obviously in a very dark place and maybe she didn't realize that it wasn't a permanent location. Maybe she didn't have support, or maybe she had the support available but didn't actually ask for help, which is even more sad.

Your particular case of postpartum blues may not be severe enough to warrant a hospital stay, but that doesn't make it any less notable. In fact, the smaller cases of baby blues can grow into something bigger if they aren't acknowledged. Sometimes just actually admitting that you are troubled is all it takes to begin the process of getting better. Carrying around sadness in silence can be exhausting and so isolating.

Be honest with yourself, your partner, and your support system during this time. Asking for help does not make you weak. Also, talk to your doctor about whether medication is the right solution for you. Some baby blues need more than fresh air and time to heal.

One of my MOFL who suffered from postpartum depression was helped tremendously by being open with those around her: "Your doctor and friends will not judge you for feeling sad. They will rally and support you! I had one girlfriend who literally took me on walks. We joked it was like she was taking her dog for a walk."

Also, if you happen to have a friend who just brought home a new baby, try to be her dog walker if you can. Let her know that you're available for anything she needs, and just go ahead and give her things you know she needs (i.e., watch the baby for an hour so she can nap, drag her along on a walk with you, bring her a delicious snack, and insist that she not change out of her pajamas when you come to visit).

You might even buy her one of my new line of pink and blue stuffed animals that have "Newborns are the worst; it's not just yours" sewn on their bellies. They are the perfect way to welcome a child home.

Journal Entry
CRAZY DAYS

I've struggled with depression throughout the years, so I braced myself for the possibility of postpartum depression hitting me following the birth of my first child. Even with that advance notice, I was still a little rattled when the baby blues showed up.

Vivian came with a lot of uncertainty. I had no clue what the hell I was doing and felt that inadequacy to my core. This was compounded by the ridiculously small amount of sleep I was getting. Then you mix in my wacky hormone levels and you are left with a blubbering mess of a new mom.

Congratulations on this exciting time!

Becky was taken aback by my completely out-of-character crying fits when my baby blues first hit. I'd never been big on emotions, and these were scaring her. But it wasn't long before she learned the correct way to help me. And that was to avoid trying to help me at all.

The first few times I randomly broke down, Becky asked me what was wrong, wanting desperately to fix it. After I repeatedly

>

answered, "I don't know!" she realized that trying to make me come up with a valid reason for my sadness was actually making me more miserable. So then we moved on to our daily question of "Is it crying time?" To which I would nod my head and start the crying. And she didn't try to fix it. It was perfect.

My sadness with Vivian had a lot to do with being overwhelmed—and the feeling that I would be overwhelmed forever. That I would never get a handle on how to be a mom, Vivian would never get a handle on how to be a person, and neither one of us would ever sleep again. These weren't rational thoughts, but I was drowning in them. I was constantly carrying around a weight of dread. I dreaded how tired I would be; I dreaded how much Vivian would be crying; I dreaded the nighttime the way a character in a horror movie dreads it. In my defense, considering the amount of screaming coming out of the child after dark, my house wasn't much different than a horror movie.

But, as babies tend to do, Vivian got bigger and easier. And I got better, in every way. Because I had dealt with depression in the past, I knew that in time I could move through it. I repeated this fact to myself over and over, when the dread was feeling endless. I asked for and accepted help. I got out of the house and forced myself to move. I buried my face in my baby's neck and breathed in her newness, even if it was her newness that was overwhelming me. I wasn't magically fixed, but over time things steadily felt better.

I had a bad case of the baby blues with Vivian, not full-on postpartum depression. It's important to note that because full-on postpartum depression cannot be cured by taking walks and breathing in your baby's newness. It requires the help of professionals and sometimes medication. If you're unsure where you fall on the scale, always err on the side of a doctor's visit to discuss options.

When Daniel was headed our way, I knew that he might bring some postpartum issues along with him as well. I braced myself for it from day one. But then it didn't hit. In fact, the opposite hit. Instead of feeling low, low, low, I felt higher than a kite.

I wasn't sure exactly what was going on, but I wasn't fighting it either. I was so damn excited to not only be done with this pregnancy but all pregnancies. I had more energy than I'd had in forty-one weeks. I was bouncing all over the place, cleaning, organizing, happy as a clam. (A clam who was seemingly unaffected by lack of sleep.)

It was odd. For someone who doesn't deviate much from the middle of the emotional scale (not too high, not too low), my manic happiness was just as noticeable as the sadness I felt with Vivian.

Neither Becky nor I knew what to make of my crazy-happy, and I think it actually hit Becky harder than the depression I had the first time. I knew what to do with the baby this time, I was crazy-happy, and I wasn't tired at all. I think Becky felt sad because she didn't feel as needed this time.

I kept telling her to wait because whatever high I was on was going to come slamming down to earth eventually. I wasn't naive enough to think it could be sustained; I was just enjoying it while it lasted.

And then one day, as I sat on the couch with no shirt on while pumping my ridiculously sore boobs (see Chapter 4:

"Breastfeeding Is Still F'n Hard"), it all came crashing down. The exhaustion slammed into me, my whole body ached from the difficulties I was having with breastfeeding, and I was pumping milk for a baby who was refusing to take a bottle for any of the hourly feedings he was demanding.

As I was sitting there trying to hold it together, Vivian walked up to me. She tilted her head while trying to figure out why exactly my boobs were being sucked into a pump. I clenched in pain with every sucking of my poor breasts into the plastic cones. Becky looked at me from across the room and asked the question that always broke me, "Are you okay?"

I was not.

I shook my head no and started to cry. Vivian's eyes grew big and she was officially concerned about how f'n crazy this house had become. Mommy was crying shirtless in the living room while getting her boobs sucked by a machine. It was probably about time to alert the authorities and shut this party down.

On cue Becky stepped up and once again helped me navigate through the postpartum sadness that blanketed me. And once again, I eventually made it though.

It turns out that postpartum euphoria is actually a thing and can be just as dangerous as postpartum depression. An emotional high can make the inevitable emotional low even more difficult. And if you're extra lucky, the whole roller coaster can result in long-term issues with bipolar disorder. Isn't making babies fun?

Postpartum euphoria is referred to as the "baby pinks" instead of the "baby blues." To me it felt more like the "baby crazies." As if I'd taken a handful of NoDoz and uppers and couldn't wait to tackle my overly ambitious To Do list. Sure, I was probably clinically insane, but damn was I productive! Maybe I finally figured out what everyone meant when they said, "Congratulations on this exciting time."

DREAM BIG

Some people spend a lot of time discussing how exciting it would be if they won the lottery.

We spend most of our time talking about how exciting it would be if our kids got up and fed themselves breakfast without our help on Saturday mornings.

*a*T SOME POINT after you bring home Baby #2, your new reality will hit you *hard*. And the reality is this: you are in way over your head.

Sometimes it hits you early and often. You'll be negotiating a poop-covered, squirming baby when you hear a trouble-seeking toddler exclaim from the other room, "Uh oh!" Or maybe you'll survive the baby days and be blindsided by your inadequacies once Child #2 becomes mobile. Because the math really starts to turn against you once you have two moving children (see Chapter 11: "1 + 1 = 54,623,452").

Activities that were once ordinary now become tests of mental and physical endurance. You think you are going to quickly drop by the store to buy a gallon of milk? Think again (see Chapter 7: "Now Is a Perfect Time to Become a Hermit"). You were planning on making an actual meal for dinner? Don't bother; the microwave was surely invented by someone with multiple children. You would like to bathe yourself or your children on a regular basis, in a manner that doesn't inspire post-traumatic stress in any of you? I recommend just hosing everyone down outside for the first couple of years to save yourself the bathroom scars.

Because Bath Time will never be the same again.

Siblings can have moments of extreme adorableness that make you beam as you observe their closeness and healthy, blossoming relationship. Then they can have moments that make you wonder if you are possibly in the beginning stages of a future *Dateline* episode (see also Chapter 9: "Your First Child Is Possibly a Psychopath").

Never will this range of emotions unfold more quickly than when two children are in a bathtub together. Maybe the warm water scrambles their brain chemistry? I'm not sure. But whatever the reason, the results are the same: bubbles gone bad. Remember how cute Child #1 was in the bath? Splishing and splashing with delight, playing with cute rubber duckies and various squirt toys? Maybe there was even some adorable bath paint involved. Oh, the bubbles, giggles, and clean body parts!

Go ahead and hold on to that memory as tightly as you can. Because it's going to become very distant as soon as Child #2 belly flops into Bath Time.

Gone are the days of innocent splashes. We have now entered the Battle of the Bath. If you are actually able to bathe both children during the Battle, you should consider yourself a tremendous success. Yes, the amount of water on the floor looks like you attempted to bathe two very large, flopping fish, but let's not focus on the negative. Also, if you were hoping to make it through the Battle without any tears shed (by the parents or the children), you were being more than a little unrealistic. Let's try to keep our goals attainable, please.

One child will want to splish and the other will want to splash. Then one will inevitably elevate the splashing to violent levels. At which point, the other child will develop a newfound and fatal allergy to water touching their body. (The allergy doesn't affect the body parts submerged in the water already. It's a very specific allergy.)

Bubbles will be introduced in an effort to broker peace. Everyone loves the bubbles. Until they don't. It was a thrilling 6.2 seconds of bubble bliss. But when the bliss ends, it is very hard to remove said bubbles from the bath. Bubbles are not meant to be destroyed, only to multiply. While one child will find this endlessly entertaining, the other will begin shrieking in agony because there are bubbles on their head and face.

In a last-ditch effort to salvage the innocence of this once delightful activity, you will bring out the bath toys. What could go wrong with bath toys, really?

The answer is everything. Everything can go wrong.

No matter how many toys there are, each child will obsess over the same rubber duck. Obviously, it's the best rubber duck; anyone can see that. Neither child can go on without this rubber duck. It is up to you to decide which child you love more, and therefore who will get the toy. And don't think you can just put the toy away. Nice try. Putting the toy away only results in inconsolable screams because, let's face it, you have ruined their entire childhoods.

So you draw an invisible line down the middle of the bath. You divide the toys. You instruct the children to play in peace on their assigned side.

They have been in the bath for only two and a half minutes at this point. You have grown four gray hairs in that time.

When the three minute mark rolls around, the children are done playing peacefully and have started throwing their toys over the imaginary line. Naked chaos ensues: splashing, ducks being fashioned into weapons, and private parts flailing about.

Bath Time is now over. You'll count the three minutes of submersion in water as cleaning the bottom half of the children. Hopefully tomorrow you can figure out a way to bathe the top halves of their bodies. But don't get too ambitious. You aren't a miracle worker.

GETTING OUT OF THE CAR IS HARD

*H*ERE'S THE THING: Amazon Prime has free shipping, and most of the things you order will get to your house in a couple of days. Amazon Now and many grocery stores will deliver essentials to your house within a couple of hours. I highly recommend you familiarize yourself with all of these services immediately. Because leaving the house with multiple children in tow is not recommended by any mental health professional.

You may be thinking that is an exaggeration, but I'm only looking out for you and your children. And for the innocent bystanders who are just trying to grab a bag of salad and don't need to see all of you huddled on the floor crying in the middle of the produce section. That is when the mental health professionals might have to get involved.

Newborns and toddlers are both just balls of disaster waiting to happen. If you are having an extra-special day you'll experience both of their disaster skills at the same time. Why on earth would you want to go into public with these kinds of people? At any given moment the toddler can begin to act like a toddler and the baby can start howling. Then you will be forced to leave both of them in the grocery store while you go start a new life in a different city. And we both know you don't have the energy to create a new identity for yourself, so let's keep things at a manageable level, shall we?

Your first clue that leaving the house is a bad idea should be the amount of effort it takes to even get out of the damn house. Before your new baby came along you might have started to hit a nice little stride with Child #1 in regard to getting out of the house in an almost functional manner. Sure, the shoes weren't always on and the child's hair sometimes looked as if a hurricane had blown by it, but the exit plan was relatively painless and could be pulled off with little to no advance warning (with an occasional assist from a sugar-laced bribe).

Now that you've added another baby to the mix, you've also added her 6,736,238 required accessories. As well as her completely unreliable crying and pooping habits. And (this is the big one) newborns are totally resistant to any and all bribing attempts. We all know your parenting victories begin and end with your ability to bribe children into doing what you want them to do.

But still, you push on. Because there has to be something better out in the real world than baby vomit and *Caillou*.

You pack up the diaper bag with bottles, cups, wipes, pacifiers, burp cloths, tissues, changing pads, backup clothes, backup clothes, backup clothes for the backup clothes, diapers, blankets, bibs, squeaky squeakers, rattling rattlers, and plenty of sugar-laced bribes. You chase Child #1 around the living room while trying to remind them how easy it used to be to leave the house. Child #1 in turn points out that you probably should have spent a little more time on the regression chapters in those baby books you were reading before Child #2 arrived.

You get the baby dressed and snap her into the car seat. Then you finally catch Child #1 and snap him into his car seat. Next you practice your weightlifting and wrestling skills by trying to fit the double stroller into the back of your car, which involves several failed attempts because the ginormous stroller only fits into the back of your car if it is at *juuuuuuuuust* the right angle. The effort is a nimble and glamorous one for all to witness. Eventually you cram the damn stroller in and violently slam the hatchback on it repeatedly, hoping to jam it into staying where it is.

After this several-minute assault on your automobile and sanity, you give up and grab the BabyBjörn. You think about grabbing the dog leash for the toddler but realize that might not be legal. By the time you get into the car, both children have gifts waiting for you. The toddler offers you a big fat meltdown that has been caused by being strapped into a chair like an animal for three minutes. And the baby has shat up her entire back.

Half an hour, a new outfit, and another round of sugary bribes later, you are back in the car and ready to go. As you pull out of the driveway you glance down at the clock and notice it is five minutes before Child #1's naptime. Thereby guaranteeing a disaster is imminent from that side of the car. You know this because in your newborn haze you've missed Child #1's naptime four times this week. Each time this has happened, you've vowed never to go down that dark road again. But keeping track of what the hell time it is can be difficult when you are barely keeping track of your sanity.

You drive around the block and get a coffee at a drive-through Starbucks and call it a successful outing. You vow to never speak ill of Caillou and his hypnotizing ways ever again.

Moms on the Front Lines

BRAVING THE GREAT OUTDOORS

I asked my MOFL about their experiences venturing out of the house with their young children. I was relieved to find that I wasn't the only one who shudders at the notion.

Colleen, mom of two boys, is not quite ready to take on the challenge: "Cody is seven months old, and I still haven't taken them both to the store alone. Ryan's a runner, and the thought of chasing him around the store with a baby on my hip scares the shit out of me."

"Runner in Aisle 5! Also, she appears to be running *away* from the toddler!"

Michelle, mom of two, used to have one sweet hour set aside for successful outings: "Actual errands by myself with the two kids didn't happen until my second was around six months old. And only between the magic hours of 11 AM and noon. Otherwise someone was having a meltdown."

Sarah G. addresses one of the biggest issues of navigating the world with a newborn and another child: "I remember being scared of needing to sit and nurse a newborn while out and about and having a 2.5-year-old that I needed to keep an eye on too. And I will add, each new kid, same fear. How will I do Costco with three? With four? But, eventually, you do it. Your kids surprise you; they're more well-mannered than you thought."

Monica, mom of four, counters that sentiment: "Ha! Right! I always realize I must have been high to think it was a good idea to take my 'nice, well-mannered' kids out."

Kaysee, however, is a show-off: "I have always been one who can't stand to stay home for long. When my second baby was born, we went to the mall when she was three days old! I always went to the park, the mall, and sometimes the office with the two of them. Talking with other adults helps me keep my sanity!"

I would need a lot of talks with adults to help me regain the sanity I lost by just getting my two kids in the car for an outing.

Michaela, mom of two, initially had a lot of success taking her two kids out and about, but lately she's turned a corner: "I've had a couple unique pleasures recently. 1. I was using a public restroom with both of them in the stall with me and my oldest escaped while my pants were around my ankles. 2. I literally dragged a kicking and screaming toddler across the floor by one arm out of a crowded coffee shop (while hauling the baby, also screaming, in the car seat in the other hand) as people watched aghast. And it escalates very quickly. One second everything is normal, and the next second the child is completely bat-shit toddler crazy (because he bit into his cookie and so now it's broken). Let's just say the honeymoon is *way* over."

Deanna, mom of three, always tried to get out into the world as soon as possible with her kids: "It was almost always hard. I always felt like I spent more time preparing for the trip than the actual trip. I have definitely had many trips where someone might not say the trip was successful. But the way I look at it is that I came home with all three kids, so that automatically equals success!"

Deanna has the right strategy when it comes to adventures outside the house. And that strategy is to have very few expectations. Your first couple of tries will be all about mastering the preparations involved in actually leaving the house with two kids. Once you have that down (probably around the time the baby is in junior high), you can raise your sights to successful outings as a member of society.

But as Deanna said, your new bar for success should be set at a ridiculously low level. I learned to declare an outing a success if I didn't have any desire to break down and cry at all during the trip. I couldn't count on my kids to go tear-free, but my goal was to slowly build up my own stamina and patience so that I could handle their crazy with a level of calm that let everyone, including the children, know that I was not going to be brought to my knees by these little people.

I would come armed with snacks and treats, iPads, and stuffed animals. I would plan my trips as far away from naptime as possible and also try to avoid places during peak busy times. There was no reason others should be exposed to our belly flops.

My kids have gotten easier as the years go on, but more than that, I've learned to be easier on all of us if we have a little hiccup along our way to functional interaction with the general public. No matter how big my kids get, I doubt I'll ever stop thinking of ways to accomplish all my intended tasks at drive-throughs. Also, if Amazon Now could start sending babysitters and basic medical services, I'd be all set.

8

YOU MAY BE
ALL OUT OF SHITS
The first kid used them all up

PLANNING AHEAD

- -

BABY #1

BABY #2

Page 1

Baby Registry

196 Cute outfits   *Bumbo*
Baby leggings   *Boppy*
Baby shoes   *Burp cloths*
Baby swing   *52 Swaddles*
Baby chair   *47 blankets*
Baby bassinet   *32 binkies*
Baby bouncer   *Wipe warmer*
Baby walker   *Bottle warmer*
Diapers   *Teething Rings*
Shopping cart cover
Nursery adorableness
Homemade baby food processor
Educational toys for newborns

Baby Due Fri.

Grab some diapers
on your way home
from work

*Y*OUR FIRST BABY brings with it a surge of maternal instincts. You must buy all the books; you must read all the blogs; you must stock up on all the items that Babies 'R' Us carries. If you don't heed the recommendations of every specialist, you are a terrible parent. Never mind that the specialists can give conflicting advice on a range of topics. That's just a way to guarantee you will feel like a failure, no matter what decisions you make. It's possible the specialists are funded by the wine industry, now that I think about it.

You may spend most of Baby #1's first months feeling overwhelmed by all the things you are surely doing wrong and by how your ineptitude will inevitably have long-term effects on your poor child.

You can't let babies sleep anywhere but their crib from day one because if you do, they will never sleep in their crib for any of their days. You aren't supposed to hold them all the time, or they will never want to be put down. You need a fourteen-page registry full of baby whatnots, or they will grow up to have the IQ of a turnip. Also, you should probably check in with the baby books every week to make sure your kid is hitting all the milestones at the appropriate times, again because of the turnip possibility. It's all so exhausting, really.

Then your second child comes along.

And by this point, you are officially out of shits. Not only have you long since realized that you were beating yourself up over nothing, but when Baby #2 barrels on to the scene you just plain won't have the time to dwell on inconsequential things (maybe leave the wipe warmers off the registry this time). Now, being out of shits doesn't mean you don't care anymore; it just means that you have brought your care down to a level that does not require high doses of medication to sustain.

And so, without further ado, I'd like to welcome you all to the Whatever Works portion of our parenting program. Pull up a chair, won't you?

Gone are the days of double and triple checking your every parenting decision. You are an old pro by now, and this go-round you aren't constantly blanketed in a sense of inadequacy. Well, you probably still feel inadequate, but you've shifted into realizing that it's not the end of the world if you aren't perfect. You and your first child have survived your parenting thus far, so you must be doing something right. Survival of all parties has moved into the number one spot on the list of your parenting goals.

When Vivian made her appearance, I seemed to spend most of my days Googling how to parent her. I was on high alert, ready to examine and stress over every noise that came out of her little body. I actually set a timer for tummy time. I was militant about following any advice I read on all the parenting blogs. With the help of WebMD, I had her diagnosed with roughly 3,526 childhood illnesses by the time she was two months old. When she wasn't sleeping enough I was worried, but then what did it mean when she was sleeping too much? That couldn't be good either.

I was a bit of a wreck—I was just so damn worried about messing this up. I was building a whole person here; there wasn't room for error! All my wrong moves would surely compound over time to absolutely ruin any shot my child had at a positive future. Although this seems less than sane now, it was completely logical to me at the time. It was more than logical; it was a fact.

And then something happened around the time Vivian turned one. She started to get a little easier. She was bigger and stronger and began to communicate more. She didn't seem so fragile, so I was able to lower the guard I constantly had up to protect her from any and all evils.

And once I relaxed a bit, I realized I had spent the first year of my child's life worrying about my failures during her current stage and agonizing over when she would move on to her next stage. Nothing about my parenting style or brain was calm. And that's an unfortunate way to spend the first months with your baby.

As Vivian got older, my go-to phrase shifted from "Oh my God!" to "Eh." I began to laugh more and stress less when the inevitable parenting hiccups occurred. Part of this was growth on my part, but most of it was just sheer exhaustion. Who has the energy to get worked up over stupid stuff?

By the time Daniel came along I was an entirely different parent than I had been when Vivian was brand-new. No longer was the fear of the unknown constantly weighing me down. This time, to some degree, I knew what was coming my way. I had been here before, and everyone had survived. I didn't think a new baby would be easy, but that wasn't the point. The point was that I knew I could survive the difficult stages, and more than anything I knew that the difficult stages were just that: stages. Everything would keep moving forward, and no stage would be permanent, even if it was a good one.

I remember my first nights with a screaming Vivian. I would bounce her around the house, trying everything in my power to calm her down and just. Get. Her. To. Sleep. It seemed as though

I would never sleep again. What if this was the type of baby she was? What if she didn't ever sleep well? It was day two, and I was already prescribing her Ambien. And then, as babies tend to do, she got better at sleeping; sometimes she would even add some nighttime hours to her repertoire. As she got older, she'd have stretches of horrible sleep because of teething or illness or the full friggin' moon. But even though those stretches felt endless, they never were.

So when Daniel had some irregular sleeping habits at the beginning, I wasn't nearly as worked up about them. This time, instead of bouncing him all around the dark house for hours while falling deeper into a pit of despair, I took a less stressful route. I illuminated the dark room with the TV and put him in his swing for a little while. Then I would take him outside and walk him up and down our block because he liked the fresh air. Then we'd do a few laps around the kitchen island and spend some time on the couch talking. It was still the middle of the night and I still wasn't sleeping, but this time around it was only the baby who wanted to scream his face off.

This time, the rules changed because we had decided early on that we were embracing the Whatever Works method of parenting. Wherever Daniel fell asleep is where Daniel stayed asleep. Early on, I spent many nights sleeping on the couch downstairs next to his swing. That was fine by me because any place I was able to sleep was a good place in my opinion. I also held Daniel longer when he fell asleep in my arms; I was not in a rush to transfer him to his crib or bassinet. But once he was awake, I was quicker to put him down. I got a play mat that had a kicking keyboard at his feet and an arch of toys over his head. He would gleefully kick and hit the toys while I gleefully accomplished actual tasks around the house, or perhaps spent some time with the other child I had birthed.

Daniel was a happy baby and relatively calm. Although he was curious, he had no interest in crawling until he was about ten months old. When Vivian wasn't crawling by eight months, I was freaking out that she would never walk. But Daniel's slow march toward mobility didn't faze me. He was developing fine, and there was a certain look in his eye that made me think I was in trouble once he figured out how to move across the room. So why rush it?

And that was my general attitude toward most things our second time around. He'll eventually walk, he'll eventually move out of his crib into a big boy bed, and he'll eventually stop crapping his pants. Let's not get ourselves worked up over it.

When I asked my MOFL whether they were more relaxed and less worried about milestones with their second baby, their answers seemed to vary based on the personality of their second child.

Sarah B. had two boys who were very similar: "Absolutely!! No child ever went to kindergarten drinking a bottle, crawling, wearing diapers!! They get there when they get there!"

Michelle's boys were polar opposites. "I am definitely more relaxed with my second child. Sometimes it's because he is my second, sometimes it's because my second is so much more mellow than my first. I don't have to be as strict because Paxton is such a chill child. I don't have to constantly stay one step ahead of him because he isn't trying to take over the world like his older brother is."

Brooke, however, had a second child who requires she give more shits: "I feel like I have to be more strict with number 2, mainly because he is a beast!!! He tests way more limits—especially my patience!"

I had a similar experience in that Daniel burst through his first birthday into a solid year and a half of crazy. His energy, mischief, and tantrums far exceeded anything I had seen from Vivian.

But because I was all out of shits, Daniel's antics didn't rock me as much as they would have if Vivian had acted the same way. We would have evenings when Daniel would get three head injuries and four time-outs in an hour because he was so out of control. But even when he was being nuts, I would just say, "Good lord, I hope this phase passes soon." I never felt overwhelmed by the thought that this child was going to be an asshole forever because I knew it would pass.

This applied to the good parts too. I never took it for granted that I got to snuggle with my boy while he breastfed. I continued doing it even past the twelve-month cut-off I had set because I knew it was a special time in his little life. And even now, although he is way too big to hold, I still gladly scoop him up and rock him to sleep in his room when he asks me to. I know it won't be long before he'll want nothing to do with my snuggles.

It's hard to imagine because of the tantrums, sleepless nights, and food whizzing past my head at every meal, but someday I will miss these times the most. Who knew that the best years of your life could be the ones filled with so many poopy diapers?

So I try to focus on the good parts of building these two little kids into functioning human beings. And I try not to give too many shits about the daily frustrations that construction effort can bring. But I have to be honest: I still consider prescribing them Ambien every damn night.

YOUR FIRST CHILD IS POSSIBLY A PSYCHOPATH

9

Jealousy is not a great look on a child

CHARACTERISTICS OF A PSYCHOTIC PERSON
(OR AN OLDER SIBLING)

PSYCHOTIC PERSON: Can be prone to fighting and aggressiveness.
OLDER SIBLING: Randomly upper cuts anyone who comes close.

PSYCHOTIC PERSON: Constantly lies and deceives others.
OLDER SIBLING: "I don't know how Baby Brother got locked in the closet."

PSYCHOTIC PERSON: Has little regard for the safety of others.
OLDER SIBLING: Has a lot of regard for demonstrating who is boss.

PSYCHOTIC PERSON: Irresponsible, can't meet financial obligations.
OLDER SIBLING: Not even looking for a job.

PSYCHOTIC PERSON: Regularly breaks or flouts the law.
OLDER SIBLING: Flouts everything, really.

PSYCHOTIC PERSON: Doesn't feel remorse or guilt.
OLDER SIBLING: But is highly skilled at fake crying.

𝒶H, YOUR FIRSTBORN. The apple of your eye. The child who defines love and adorableness. Isn't he or she the best?

I'm sorry to inform you that there is a real possibility that this child is a psychopath. There, lurking beneath the surface (don't let that button nose and those bouncy curls fool you) is an evil you never knew existed. But don't worry; you'll see it soon enough.

The moment you bring another kid into the house, Child #1 will be on a Countdown to Terror. He will be biding his time, waiting for just the right moment to show the world his true colors. Or maybe your precious daughter will be gazing at the newborn while thinking, "A little less sugar and a little more spice is going to be needed to deal with this new baby."

The evil can reveal itself early on or can pop up in the middle of what you thought was a beautiful, blossoming sibling relationship. Either way, when the psychotic behavior starts, that sibling relationship takes a bit of a dark turn.

Maybe your older child will be upset that this new baby has stolen the spotlight, so they will deem it necessary to assail the newborn's head with a stuffed elephant. Or maybe Child #1 doesn't mind having a newborn around but is not so fond of their sibling becoming coordinated enough to reach for Child #1's favorite toys ("favorite toys" being any toys within a three-mile radius of the house). Child #1 just may sprint across the room and body slam Child #2 as soon as there is even an innocent glance toward any toy.

This behavior will leave you baffled and also convinced that your child has somehow morphed into an evil being. How did this happen? Child #1 was so calm and cute! And now they are, without a hint of hesitation or remorse, causing harm to Child #2. Images of Macaulay Culkin in *The Good Son* flash before your eyes (spoiler alert: the son didn't turn out to be very good).

I reached out to a therapist for some insight into this descent into darkness, and it turns out our kids actually *are* psychopaths, or at least demonstrate similar characteristics. That's comforting.

Licensed clinical social worker Gail Marie Poverman-Kave explains, "A very important thing for parents to understand is that prior to age six or seven, children really don't have a grasp of the concept of 'other.' We may believe that they understand the difference between right and wrong; however, they do not. That requires frontal lobe activity and the frontal lobe doesn't kick into gear until about six or seven. We mistakenly ascribe our thinking onto the toddler, believing that his or her actions are genuinely malicious or deliberately cruel when in reality they are basic cause and effect. Sometimes they are looking for the baby to react in some fashion but unfortunately a parent's over-the-top response can be even more enjoyable."

So maybe you shouldn't scream, "Why are you trying to kill your sibling?!!" when Child #1 acts aggressively toward the new baby. It turns out that might not help the situation.

Instead, Poverman-Kave recommends offering positive alternatives to your child's psychotic behavior and redirecting them toward the light when things go off-track: "Praise your older child for all positive behaviors and avoid punishing for misbehavior. Punishing the child for negative behaviors will only reinforce them."

This seems like a really good idea in theory, but it is difficult to execute when your kid is being an asshole. I can't say I've ever been very good at keeping calm in the face of bad behavior, but

I have made a conscious effort to praise good behavior. I take the time to note the good: "Thank you for playing so nice with your brother; I really appreciate it." Or maybe something like, "Thanks for not being an asshole today! That was so fun." You know, to keep it positive.

I asked my MOFL about their experiences with Culkin-like behavior, and they told me they've seen it at different stages in their children's sibling relationships.

Michaela, mom of two, had issues early on: "We had some rough times in the beginning. I couldn't safely leave Sam in the room with the baby. I caught him in the pack 'n' play with her a number of times and lots of hard slaps on the head, hair pulling, lying on her like a pancake, and just generally trying to kill her, either on purpose or accidentally."

I remember when Michaela was going through this and she reached out to the other MOFL for advice. She was upset and didn't know what to do. I witnessed Sam smack his sister once, and he was all smiles before, during, and after the hit. What I could see, and what I tried to explain to comfort Michaela, was the fact that Sam was not being malicious. He was just a two-year-old boy who was really interested in the cause and effect of smacking this little baby. Just as my two-year-old went through a phase of pulling the cat's tail because it seemed to get the cat and his parents to react.

Poverman-Kave goes back to the concept of "other" to explain why the kids don't understand that they are causing pain: "They can't feel what you feel and haven't developed empathy yet, so expecting them to understand these things is unfair to them and frustrating for all involved."

Frustrating is one word for it; horrified is another.

Dana, mom of two, was shocked when her firstborn snapped: "Rory was about five days old and Reese smacked him in the head out of nowhere. I almost died and cried. The first four days prior had gone so well, so I was stunned."

Jen, also a mom of two, had her experience with psychosis when her baby was a bit older. "I literally could not leave Austin alone in the room with Maddyn when she got to the crawling stage. She would go after his toys and he would try to take her out! Poor girl suffered many tackles, body slams, bites, and even a black eye from him stabbing her in the eye with his toothbrush. I would have to put up a baby gate to keep them separate for a while. It was a rough phase that lasted only a few weeks. Now they are besties!"

It's important to remember that this behavior is usually temporary. It can seem endless because it's absolutely baffling how many times you have to demonstrate "gentle hands" to the child. It's not really a difficult concept to grasp, kid. And why are you looking at me as if this is the first time we've had this discussion? Are you blocking out the talks we had five, ten, and fifteen minutes ago?

Eventually this phase, like every other one your kid goes through, will pass. Try to keep reminding yourself of this when the phase feels particularly long term. If you find yourself growing tired of having to repeatedly ask your child to act like a civilized human being, then it might be best to take Jen's advice and separate the kids periodically. Or at least separate the demon child from you if you feel yourself crossing over to the dark side as well.

Over the years I've perfected my "silent removal" of an offending child. I don't say anything; I don't let the loud screams in my head come out of my mouth; I just pick up the kid and take them to a designated "You are driving me crazy" location. This action usually results in plenty of screaming from the child, but there is no interaction with me once the child is there. When my child is driving me crazy, I walk away so I won't end up starring in a *Dateline* episode about a loving mom who snapped.

As you navigate your way through this lovely phase, try to find your own equivalent of a "You are driving me crazy" location— a go-to reaction to help you stay calm when your child is exhibiting psychotic behavior. Maybe you remind her to use "gentle hands," maybe you redirect him to something positive, or maybe you pour yourself a glass of wine and huddle in the corner. You know, common parenting tactics.

Journal Entry

VIVIAN'S DARK SIDE

When my sweet Vivian began showing signs of psychosis, I was so confused. She had always been such a gentle child. She was shy and reserved and didn't act out very often. But as soon as her brother started crawling, it became apparent that she had been keeping a dark secret from us for years: she's fully prepared to go apeshit on anyone who dares to touch her toys.

Vivian started throwing Daniel sideways glances as soon as he stopped being simply a blob of cute who did nothing but blob in one place all day. Her gentle touches became decidedly less friendly when she noticed him moving in the direction of her toys. Initially, she would simply get to the toys faster than he would, and he would get frustrated. Those were the simple times.

Then he started to move more quickly, and she wasn't able to maintain an adequate defense on all toy fronts. He would finally get his hands on a toy, and *BAM!* she would knock it out of his hands. As his coordination grew, so did her attacks. From the corner of her eye she would spot him having the audacity to pick up one of her toys, and the next thing I knew she was sprinting across the room to grab it from him. She would also throw in a nice push to the ground as a consequence for his trespassing.

I would repeatedly tell her that she needed to share and that she needed to be nice to her brother. I would point out that we had enough toys for everyone in the free world to have one, so maybe being possessive over every single one was overkill. I would demonstrate how a sane person is supposed to react when her toy is being touched by a baby. Not only was she not listening, but she seemed to be getting more methodical in her approach.

Instead of simply pushing the boy down, she started hip-checking him as she walked by and then would look at me the way an NFL player looks at a ref when he can't *believe* a flag has been thrown against him on that play: "I didn't *mean* to, Mommy! It was an accident!" That's when we started moving into Culkin territory.

She was always three steps ahead of her brother, and she would use those three steps to devise an appropriate punishment for his crimes. Almost all punishments resulted in his tears and her time-out. As she got more skilled she would incorporate her own tears, in the hope that she could pin some of the blame on her brother by claiming, "He hitted me!"

Unfortunately for Vivian, and despite my promises that this was coming, Daniel kept growing bigger, stronger, and faster. And, thanks to Vivi kicking his ass early and often, he was also getting pretty tough. As he's grown, he has been able to match and even exceed her apeshit abilities at a remarkably young age. It's been such a delight to see their sibling relationship mature into this exciting phase (see Chapter 17: "Siblings Aren't Nearly as Adorable as You Imagined").

I would like to say that Vivian's antics were short-lived and disappeared as she got older, but that wouldn't be an accurate assessment of the current situation in my household. Yes, our days are now filled with more good behavior than bad, but Vivian still has flashes of jealousy and possessiveness that snap her brain into Evil Mode. However, now that Daniel has gotten bigger, I don't worry as much about him being picked on because he can more than stand up for himself. In fact, these days they spend most of their time taking turns going apeshit. It's just lovely.

My absolute favorite is when I hear a child crying and I round the corner to investigate. I point to the child who is in a heap of tears and ask, "What happened? Did you hurt him?" The other child, with a huge grin on her face, shakes her head and says innocently, "Nope."

We will need to go to the instant replay on this one.

HOW CHILDREN AFFECT YOUR FACE

Your face when you have children and get 4 hours sleep.

Your face when you have children and get 8 hours sleep.

Your face when you are on a girls' weekend away from your children and get 3 hours sleep.

$\mathcal{L}$ET'S START OUT by saying that you are beautiful. Your body MADE human beings. From scratch. There was a chapter in those pregnancy books that said your children were at one point the size of a pea inside you. Not only did you grow that pea into a person (that must be the miracle part they always talk about), but you then negotiated that person out of your body in one way or another.

You're a farkin' warrior.

But, and here's the bad news, warriors have scars to show for their battles. And they also have really saggy boobs, it turns out. You'll find that the more battles you've seen, the worse your scars will get. And the more the boobs will sag.

The state of your body following Baby #2 might come as a bit of a shock because that isn't how things looked after Baby #1. I'm sorry to inform you that your body is officially done with your shenanigans, and things are about to turn a corner.

Your body may have forgiven you after Baby #1. It may have thought that this person-making adventure was a fluke, an accident, even. If you were lucky, your various parts might have gone back to their general pre-gestation locations. Maybe you dodged stretch marks and were able to escape with little evidence that your womb was the site of an alien-like reproduction experiment. You were given a bit of a pass because surely you wouldn't ever put your body through something that gnarly again.

And then you went and blew everything up for a second time (literally). And now your body is pissed (if you have bladder issues, this might also be literal).

This time there will be consequences. And if you decide to keep up this nonsense by making even more children, it's just going to keep getting uglier. Consider your jiggly belly a warning shot of sorts.

This go-round, things won't bounce back the way they did before. In fact, gravity has officially become your enemy, and bouncing is no longer part of your body's repertoire. Your body is, however, really excelling at the plummeting-to-the-ground part of the bouncing equation. So there's that.

I asked my MOFL about their destroyed bodies, and it turns out that we are a mangled bunch.

Carrie, mom of two, agreed that Baby #2 was a tipping point: "My body definitely took a turn down a wrong path after #2. I was so glad that I made it through #1 without any major lasting effects. Then with #2 I got everything: the stretch marks, spontaneous urination, sagging boobs, the whole package."

And what a lovely package it is.

Sarah B., mom of two, has acknowledged that nothing will ever look the same: "It definitely took longer to lose and keep off weight after #2. I feel like my body's natural weight was reset for an extra five pounds. My boobs are little and sad. And the skin on my stomach looks normal when I am standing completely upright, but has a crepe-like appearance if I bend at all. Damn kids. So worth it."

I understand what Sarah means about the crepe belly, but I think her belly is in better shape than mine because mine looks more like a thick, folded pancake. Actually, more like pancake batter. With lumps.

Erika had some issues that required medical intervention: "I had surgery to stop peeing myself after pregnancy #2 when it didn't get any better after a year of Kegels and all kinds of other supposed fixes. Best decision I ever made!"

You just don't know **glamour until you** are shopping for diapers for the baby and mommy **at the same** time.

Debbie, mom of five, thinks we should all be allowed a tummy tuck and a boob job after our final kid: "I remember when I was in the shower with my two-year-old and she asked why my boobs were melting."

We all ask ourselves the same question every time we get in the shower, kid. It took a miracle to bring them down, and we are going to need another miracle (of the surgical variety) to get them back up where they belong.

Moms on the Front Lines

THAT TIME OF THE MONTH

One of the consequences of multiple pregnancies that isn't discussed much is the effect they can have on your periods. After I had Daniel, my period took over a year to come back, even after I stopped breastfeeding. When it finally did come back it wasn't consistent, and it was accompanied by the feeling that my entire body was being wrung out for several days before and during my actual period. I was beyond exhausted. When I asked my doctor about it, she said it could be a while before my body got back on track, and it wasn't worrisome that my cycle had no idea how to cycle correctly.

I wanted to see if I was the only one to suffer from period issues, and once again my MOFL did not disappoint in sharing their experiences. Most of them are done having kids, and consequently many of their husbands have had vasectomies. Those women are also experiencing their first periods off birth control.

Kaysee, mother of three, felt that her periods got progressively worse after each pregnancy: "My period came back within about four months with each child because I did not produce enough milk and had to do a lot of pumping and supplementing. I do not remember my period being so heavy before. I think birth control helped with my symptoms prior to having kids. I now get so tired and have terrible cramps in my back and stomach a few days before and during! I usually have at least one day where I feel like I can barely handle my kids or even my life! TMI?"

Erika had to go searching for her period after her last pregnancy: "Mine took over two years to come back after my second baby (I breastfed for a year). That was after two rounds of estrogen (that didn't work) and finally acupuncture and voodoo magic. Now I'm on a twenty-five-day cycle, which is not awesome."

After hearing about all of our lost periods, **Carrie** felt cheated: "I got my period back after about five months with both of my kids. Even though I exclusively breastfed with both babies. I definitely got screwed in the period reprieve."

Carrie coined a new phrase for what happened to her when she stopped taking her birth control pill after her second child: "My periods are crazy heavy, but only two days. It's like my body wants to speed dump all my innards. Ladies beware. Vasectomy + no pill + midthirties = speed dumping. You're welcome!"

Sarah seconded the speed dump description: "Yes! This is me post #3 and #4. Although I suspect it has more to do with age and perimenopause than pregnancy. This didn't occur after my

>

first two children that I had in my twenties. In my late thirties and post-vasectomy (no pill), I'm a speed dumper too."

Sarah just mentioned perimenopause, which means she is calling us all old, which means she is now no longer part of our group. We don't need that kind of negativity around here.

Monica's period has been all over the place since having kids: "After my first baby, I got my period back at eight months. Then I got pregnant two months later. I had the Mirena IUD put in after my second baby. It was tricky. Most of the time I'd get no period. Then there was this time I bled for twelve weeks straight. After I got it taken out, I bled immediately. And it took almost a year to get pregnant. After my third child, my period came back around seven months. I got pregnant two months later. After my last baby, I got the Mirena again. I didn't love it. I had it removed and got the copper IUD put in. I bled like crazy the first few periods. I'm talking over ten tampons a day. Good times!"

When I heard Monica's story, I instantly imagined what it would be like if men had to endure the period struggles that we do. Monica had a pretty spot-on description of how that switch would play out: "My husband would probably drive to ER each month."

In this small sample of women, we have cases of not getting your period back for years, of bleeding way too early, and of dumping all your innards every month in a forty-eight-hour bloodbath. The point is, periods vary widely, so keep an eye on yours and talk to your doctor about anything that doesn't seem right.

And then be prepared to be shocked when your doctor just shrugs and says, "Yeah, that happens." Who knew uteruses were so moody?

Journal Entry

THE AFTERMATH

I got really lucky with my first pregnancy. And by lucky I mean sick. I lost a lot of weight in my first couple of trimesters, so by the end I hadn't gained very much weight overall. Afterward, without doing much besides breastfeeding, I was back to my pre-pregnancy weight quickly, and my body wasn't really worse for the wear. Unless you count my poor breastfeeding boobs. They've been down and out for a while.

After Daniel came along, I was able to take weight off pretty easily because I breastfed him for a year. Breastfeeding has been known to help women lose pregnancy weight because it burns quite a few calories (at least those bleeding nipples are good for something). But, I also continued to eat healthy foods and didn't drink soda while my body was feeding the baby. Yet another factor limiting the food I could eat while breastfeeding was that both of my kids had reactions to certain foods. For instance, when I ate Mexican food or pizza Daniel got an upset belly, so I had to avoid both for the year he was on the boob. It was such a confusing time, to be so happy to have a new baby and so sad to have lost my precious soda and nachos.

But then, after ten months of pregnancy and thirteen months of breastfeeding Daniel, I got back control of my body. There was no longer a baby inside or attached to the outside of me! I did not have to hesitate when deciding what to eat or drink. I was free to pollute my body as I saw fit!

>

Not surprisingly, that's when things started to go a little off-course in the weight management department.

I told myself I wasn't going to resume my Mountain Dew/caffeine habit after I stopped breastfeeding because soda is horrible for you. Obviously I am strong enough to go without it, as I had demonstrated for the past two years. I had turned over a new leaf! I was strong in body and mind!

That leaf stayed turned over for approximately twelve hours. My weakness kicked in when I spotted a soda machine across the way during my first restaurant visit after I stopped breastfeeding. It was all downhill from there. I spent the next couple of weeks drinking soda like a drug addict on a bender. My body once again had carbonated bubbles and high-fructose corn syrup coursing through its veins, and I experienced the most glorious caffeine high as a result.

My body also had nachos and pizza and salsa and French fries rattling around too. I was like Tom Hanks after he got off that island in *Cast Away*. I had spent two years on a sad little island that was populated by only salads and water. Now I had made my way back to the mainland, which was littered with calories, fat, and caffeine. It was such a delightful time.

You're going to be shocked to find out that I put on a little weight following this rebellion against my own health. And although it wasn't a ton of weight it has stayed on, mostly in the stomach and ass. My twice-stretched-out stomach just doesn't forgive a few extra pounds the way it used to. Now I constantly look about three months pregnant. With twins.

I've flirted with trying to exercise my extra weight away, but those plans are always derailed when I remember that eating ice cream on the couch while watching Netflix is a much more enjoyable way to spend my child-free time. You see my dilemma.

But my current look isn't all bad. For instance, Daniel can be entertained for quite some time by simply sitting on my lap and pushing on my belly as if it's Play-Doh he is trying to mold into some sort of exciting shape. And lord knows how hard it is to get that boy to sit still for longer than a few minutes.

"Mommy has a squishy belly!"

"She does, buddy. Now you sit still while I finish eating this mint chip ice cream and ensure that you never have to deal with a stomach that has defined ab muscles. How boring would that be?"

1 + 1 = 54,623,452

The most unfortunate math

RELATIONSHIPS
BEFORE KIDS

RELATIONSHIPS
AFTER KIDS

*a*DDING A NEW child to your house seems like an easy enough notion. You've done this before, so you'll be able to do this again. What could go wrong?

The answer to that question is: everything. Everything can go wrong.

Have you ever heard the expression "going ass over tea-kettle?" That phrase, and its imagery of someone falling/flailing with her ass over her head, is a pretty good way to describe how you are going to look and feel once you add another child to your brood. It's not a great look.

You were expecting the addition of a child to work like the math you learned in school, where one child plus one child would equal two children. But making assumptions of any sort in regard to children is just asking for trouble. Because children don't like assumptions. And they have no time for your math. They are too busy planning the next way to make you openly weep.

Try to be realistic when envisioning the amount of work, noise, headaches, exhaustion, juggling, and patience you are going to experience as a parent of multiple children. Because adding another child to the equation does so much more than simply double everything. If you are looking for an accurate equation, take your current amount of work, noise, headaches, exhaustion, juggling, and patience and multiply it by roughly 54,623,452. That ought to give you a good idea of what is coming.

Amy, one of my MOFL, is a math teacher, but she still can't explain how the numbers go so terribly wrong with the addition of another child: "Why doesn't everything just double? So it would take you twice as long to get out of the house? No . . . quadruple it. On a good day. I don't get it."

An extra-special aspect of sibling math is that the equation changes constantly, based on circumstances you will never fully understand. Why do the kids sometimes act like complete angels and then other times act like wild banshees? What makes one child switch over to banshee while the other one is still rooted in angelic? How could a routine that worked so well yesterday have such catastrophic results today? And why did you just walk into the room to find one child with no pants, the other child covered in Desitin, the dog wearing a tiara, and everyone in tears? Don't bother trying to understand any of this because children aren't big on logic, and now that you have more than one of them, your life will never make sense again.

In our case the multiple children struggles didn't hit us as hard as I expected in the beginning. Sure, there was a completely new person in our house, and this time the overwhelming needs of a newborn had to be met alongside the equally noteworthy demands of our toddler. But even with that delightful combo platter of obligation, Baby #2 still didn't feel as overwhelming as Baby #1 had.

There are two reasons for this. The first and most important reason was that we were already well-rooted in exhaustion long before the second baby arrived. When Vivian made her appearance the shock to our system was similar to how you feel the first day back to work after a relaxing two-week vacation (in my case the vacation had been about thirty-three years). But with Baby #2, I just felt like my boss had asked me to work overtime on a Friday after a crazy workweek (a week that also included me giving birth, incidentally).

The Freedom and Regular Sleep Patterns Ship had sailed two years before, so Daniel's arrival didn't take our legs out from

---

underneath us quite the way Vivi's had. She had already knocked us to the ground and kept us down there.

The second reason Daniel didn't instantly destroy us upon arrival was that he couldn't actually move when he first got here. Some may say that babies need time to grow and evolve into functioning humans. But I say that is nature's way of giving parents a little time to adjust.

What if human babies were like those foals you see in YouTube videos, popping out and running around five minutes later? Oh, hell no. Even if you are an atheist, you have to believe in a God who was smart enough to know that humans couldn't survive such a thing.

"But God, every other animal is walking very soon after birth."

"Yes, I know, but humans need several months to prepare for their baby's mobility. They need to work up to such things. We can't have human babies running around the streets. Their parents will be way too tired to chase after them in the beginning."

"Okay, God, but can we still create tiny shoes for babies, even though they don't actually walk?"

"That I will allow."

And so it was.

HAVING A NEWBORN and a toddler wasn't exactly smooth sailing, but looking back on it now, I really should have valued Daniel's time spent in one spot. I had no idea that those were the glory days.

I could put him in his swing or on his floor mat and run Vivian to the bathroom. Or if I was ambitious, I could make or eat a quick meal without having to worry about where Daniel would be when I returned. It was a simple time, really.

Yes, having to lug around a new baby and his baby whatnots was less than convenient, but at least none of his baby whatnots were running away from me.

Once Daniel became mobile, my 1 + 1 equation started multiplying at an alarming rate.

Have you ever seen people trying to catch a chicken? They are hunched over, running and grabbing, lurching forward, but trying to avoid falling at the same time. That is how I look and feel pretty much every day in my house. Except I have two chickens, and I'm pretty sure they are working together to outsmart me. Which, admittedly, is not a difficult goal for the chickens. Because Mommy Chicken has officially gone ass over teakettle.

You may think that adding in another adult would balance this equation. Becky and I should have developed a man-to-man defense to contain our chickens. But if you believe that, then I need to remind you to picture two people in that chicken coop trying to catch those two chickens. Are you picturing a lot of running into each other and quite a few face-plants while the chickens merrily scurry around? Because that's what you should be picturing.

As the kids get older I have glimmers of them someday playing peacefully together or—and this is probably wishful thinking—entertaining themselves independently in two entirely different rooms of the house. A coop gone quiet would be a dream come true.

Most of the time these glimmers are shattered by one or both of the children deciding that peace and tranquility are an unacceptable state of being. In an instant my home goes from being the scene of a Pottery Barn photoshoot to a heavy metal concert. And all of a sudden, I have to become a large security guard trying to keep the drunk people from ending up in the hospital.

If you are reading this before your second child has started moving across the room, I implore you to do everything in your power to delay this development. Bring all toys to within arm's reach of the child. Put him in very slippery clothes that make getting up on all fours difficult (or even put roller skates on his feet to make sure he can't ever get up). Keep him in that baby swing until age nineteen. And avoid tummy time at all costs.

As soon as that kid starts moving, you might as well lie down on the ground and let him crawl all over you. Because that's where this is heading.

Moms on the Front Lines

DATE NIGHT: KID EDITION

One way to cut down on the craziness that multiple children bring to your house is to separate the children whenever possible. We find that moving the kids to different parts of the house provides a welcome respite for everyone.

Each parent plays with her assigned child, and peace descends upon the home. The kids love the one-on-one time, and the parents love that no one is putting anyone in a headlock. It's a win for all of humanity, really.

In addition, taking each child out individually for dates with one or both parents can provide a break from the normal chaos of siblings. It's baffling how good the kids are when they are not focused solely on getting into or out of a headlock. They act like completely different children, which can make conversations and calm dining experiences a possibility. I'm not sure why they need to be separated from each other for that to be possible, but let's not dwell on the details.

I asked my MOFL if they try to get one-on-one time with their kids, and their answers ranged from "I should" to regularly scheduled date nights.

Brooke sneaks in quality time when the opportunity arises: "We don't do it as often as we should, but when the older kiddo gets invited to a birthday party it's always fun to leave early and have a coffee date or girl time. When the older one is at preschool, I enjoy park or play time with the younger one. He loves it!"

Michelle also spends a lot of time with her youngest son while her older boy is in school, so she makes a point to plan time alone with her firstborn: "I do date night with my son. He picks where we go to dinner. He loves the one-on-one time and is really well-behaved."

I've often been tempted to do date night every night because the kids are so well-behaved.

Jen struggles to make time: "It's hard now, being a single mom. I always have them both. Sometimes, if I can pick up my daughter from school a little early, we will do a quick 'girl date.' Starbucks cake-pop for her, coffee for mom. And amazing conversation!"

Kaysee has monthly dates with her kids, but she likes the little moments as well: "My middle daughter even thinks it is special when we ride somewhere together and just turn off the music and talk without the distraction of her other two siblings."

Jen and Kaysee both note a fun result of one-on-one time: conversation. We've noticed that too, especially with Vivian. Having our undivided attention allows her to dominate a conversation without any effort. I love these conversations with her, whether it's while we are out to eat or alone at night right before bed. They give me a little glimpse into her brain that is otherwise drowned out by sibling noise.

Jill and her husband go on dates with their two children but also find ways within the house to spend time with them: "We do homework individually with them to let them feel individual attention at that time."

Rachel, mom of twins, doesn't have many moments alone with her kids, so she grabs them when she can: "With twins, a trip to the grocery store one-on-one can be special. So can the twenty minutes before the second kid wakes up. Every snuggle or book read is one-on-one time; you just take it where you can get it!"

Jill and Rachel make a good point that spending time alone with your kids doesn't require elaborate planning. Tiny moments here and there allow you the opportunity to focus solely on one child and give that child all your attention for a little while. Try to grab onto those moments when you see them, let them last a little longer than they should. You'll be amazed at what you can find out about your children when they know they have your full attention.

The most exciting discovery is that they are actually able to communicate in ways that don't involve screaming at the top of their lungs. Who knew?

BEST RADIO STATION EVER

- -

- -

I AM HEARING IMPAIRED and an only child. Up until I had kids my life was pretty quiet. More important, until I had kids I had control over the noise level. Besides my yippy dog barking at every (mostly imagined) enemy, my home was a place of tranquility and calm.

Vivian excised that Zen almost immediately upon her arrival. Nothing shatters tranquility quite like a newborn who won't stop crying at 2 AM (and 3 AM, and 4 AM, and really, all the AM's). And lord have mercy on the yippy dog if his yips caused the baby to start crying.

As Vivian got older, the noise level in our house started to go down a little. We still heard the normal kid sounds, but even those were at a lower level because Vivian was such a reserved child.

All was calm. All was bright.

Then I decided I'd had enough of that.

Having multiple children is a roller coaster of emotions. Most of those emotions relate directly to how loud the children are at any given second. When both kids are peacefully quiet, you experience a level of serenity that far exceeds anything any New Age teacher has ever been able to impart (bonus Zen points if this serenity results from both children sleeping at the same time). It is in those moments that you finally understand everything Oprah has ever said on SuperSoul Sunday.

And then, with little to no advance notice, your thoughts switch from Zen to Zin when both children start crying at the same time (bonus misery points if this symphony of suffering occurs in a public place). It is in those moments that you question every life decision that led you to this horrible place in time— while reaching for the corkscrew.

In the beginning, Daniel brought the normal baby sounds along with him. They weren't great, but you couldn't really blame the kid for crying as that was his only way to communicate any and all of his needs.

The real noise kicked in a little later, when Daniel got old enough to play with Vivian. And I've found that it just keeps getting noisier, with the day he learned how to talk marking the biggest spike in noise to date. Now I have two kids talking at great length about everything and absolutely nothing twenty-four hours a day. (Literally. These children wake up in the middle of the night talking about who knows what because their little mouths just can't stop moving even when they are in the middle of their REM sleep pattern.) And since neither child is interested in being a polite human, the stories are told at exactly the same time, with each one of them trying to be just a little bit louder than the other.

Not that actual vocabulary is necessary for Daniel to make noise. Most of the time his stories include elaborate gibberish and hand gestures that remind me of an old Italian man speaking to his buddies in Sicily.

Don't hold your breath for the children to run out of stories and go silent because talking is not necessary for their other primary noise-making activity: playing. Playing and screaming go hand in hand. You aren't really playing with someone if you aren't making more noise than they are. It's a rule. It's okay to play by yourself quietly but absolutely unacceptable to interact with another child without attempting to break the sound barrier. Another rule.

The more children you have, the louder it will get in your once peaceful home. But—and here is the math you forgot to take into consideration—each new child will also bring along the most dreaded of additions: friends. Try to avoid them if at all possible. Socialization is overrated.

Even if you have only two kids, and each has only one friend, you are now looking at a house with four kids in it. And that shit can break your damn eardrums.

In my very scientific independent studies I've found that the noise level goes up ten decibels with each additional child. Also, the pitch rises from "normal" to "dogs a block away are howling" as more kids are added. I'm not sure why groups of small children seem to communicate primarily via screeches, but I think it has something to do with them being annoying.

Each one needs to talk/scream louder than the last one in order to be heard. Meanwhile, the only sounds your brain hears come through like the noise Charlie Brown's teacher makes. That is, if Charlie Brown's teacher were screaming like a wild banshee with a bunch of other teachers-turned-banshees.

Another reason to avoid socializing your kids: each one of those friends will have a birthday party once a year. And each one of those birthday parties will be held in a place that is louder than the last. In addition to the unbearable noise level, those parties will also require you to bounce and/or play Whac-A-Mole while your brain slowly seeps out of your ears from overstimulation. Death by Chaos is the technical term for it, I think.

The only real advice I have for you with regard to this debilitating issue is to somehow arrange massive hearing loss as I have. I didn't develop the hearing loss as a coping mechanism after I had children, but it sure has come in handy. It may seem like an unfortunate disability, but there is nothing more pleasant than sitting down on the couch, planting a fake smile on my face, and popping out my hearing aids while the children screech their way through the popular game "Run and Screech." Mommy prefers her game called "Deaf and Happy."

All is calm. All is bright.

NOW YOU GET TO FAIL TWO KIDS INSTEAD OF JUST ONE

Plenty of guilt to go around!

A BRIGHT FUTURE AHEAD

*T*HE OTHER DAY I was in the bathroom attending to lady business. Vivian pushed open the door to ask me something. I closed the door and told her I would be right out. When I got out of the bathroom I found her crying in the corner of my room, her face buried in her hands. I asked her what was wrong, and she wailed, "You hurt my feelings!" I responded, "I'm sorry, sweetie, I just wanted privacy, like you want privacy sometimes when you're in the bathroom." She was beyond consolation at that point.

Later it occurred to me that this interaction was a pretty spot-on example of what it means to be a parent. I'd just gotten the kids out of the shower; they had dried off and were running toward their rooms with Becky to get dressed for bed. I thought that this would be a good time to attend to lady business. As soon as the thought entered my mind I ran into the bathroom because I had been alone for going on twelve seconds, and this solitude wouldn't last much longer. Anything over ten seconds is borrowed time; everyone knows that.

And then, not *five* seconds into my business, Vivi's little face appeared, needing something. And that's parenthood in a nutshell: little faces always needing something, and you destroying their entire childhoods if you take more than ten seconds away from meeting those needs.

Now, obviously, that is a dramatic take on things, but in that moment of lady business and so many other moments throughout my days, it certainly feels true.

We all know that having kids means shifting our focus toward something and someone other than ourselves. That is not an unexpected development. In fact, many would argue that it's exactly the gig we signed up for. And it is. But that doesn't make the gig any easier.

Since day one of parenthood, I've constantly felt over-whelmed by all the things I should be doing or should be doing better. Bringing Daniel into the equation seemed to overload my already maxed out brain. Now I was able to fail two kids instead of just one! What an exciting time!

Daniel's voice became one more in my household calling my name. "Mommy!" "Mommy!" "Mommy!" On particularly try-ing days, that name can sound like nails on a chalkboard. Because each time it is screamed, it has a need attached to it. And rarely do I feel that I'm able to meet all those needs with the attention they deserve.

I was an only child and didn't really settle down into a rela-tionship until I was in my thirties. This meant I had a lot of "me time" for the first thirty of my years. As an adult, I spent this time building a writing and graphic design career. I worked long hours, did projects for free to improve my portfolio, and gener-ally kicked ass professionally. I was good at what I did and I took pride in that fact.

Once I had Vivian, my focus shifted. I still worked, but I felt less driven than I had previously, partly because of sheer exhaus-tion, but mostly because work lost some of its importance once my child came along. Now I wanted to kick ass at being her mom, and that meant kicking less ass at professional endeavors.

The only problem with this plan was that I couldn't and didn't want to quit working. So now I had to split my time between work and family. People do that every day, so it should not have been a problem for me. And if you were to look at my work and the health and well-being of my daughter, you wouldn't think it was a problem.

But when I looked at both, I saw something glaring. I wasn't kicking ass at either. For someone who always prided herself on being very good, I was constantly hovering around mediocre. And I've pretty much stayed in that location ever since.

That's not to say I've done poorly at work or been a bad mom to my kids. It's just that I always have a lingering feeling that I could be doing better all around. That if I just had a little more time, a little more sleep, I could give everything and everybody what they deserve.

Even after I get the children quietly in their beds for the night, I still have four other creatures vying for my attention. The cats and dogs can't actually scream "Mommy!" but they get their point across by finding a way to put their entire bodies on top of mine as soon as I lie down in my bed.

Now, don't get me wrong. I love each of these humans and animals. I'm sharing a home and a life with them because they are my family. I would do anything for them (except, perhaps, allow all the animals to sleep on top of me as they would prefer). But I think that's what makes the chorus of *Mommy!* so overwhelming. How do I answer them all?

How do I give each of them what they deserve? How do I prioritize and divvy up my attention to everyone? What do I let slip through the cracks because there just aren't enough hours in the day (or at least, not enough caffeine to keep me awake for enough of those hours)? And where do I possibly fit in everything I need to do for work?

When there is only one me.

It can all be very overwhelming and more than a little confusing. When did this happen? How did I become a grownup who is responsible for running a household? I still feel like the twenty-year-old kid who spent quite a few years sleeping on a futon in a cheap apartment. I once lived primarily on Mountain Dew and bags of salad, and now I'm responsible for the well-being and growth of actual humans. Who thought I was qualified to do this?

I asked my MOFL if they too feel overwhelmed by everything that is required of them on a daily basis. It turns out we are all in way over our heads.

Kaysee has a house full of three kids, a husband, and her mother, so she is juggling a lot: "I am always overcommitting myself. I still stay very involved with our business, work in my kids' classes every week, and I feel like I am always driving to one activity or another with kids who are involved in way too many activities. I love my children more than anything in the world, but there are days I wish I could clone myself to get everything done and give everyone the attention that they need!"

Sarah G., mom of four, is the one who runs her household: "I am definitely the one who keeps the wheels on: bills paid, class donations, field trip forms, school supplies, auto maintenance, homework done, etc. Plus, I work. Yes, I feel overwhelmed occasionally. But the emotion I experience more is failure. Like, I don't think my fourth child has been to the doctor for a year. He doesn't get sick and I don't remember well-child visits. Or, my nine-year-old has one pair of pants; that's it. I just don't remember to shop for him!"

Sometimes that "To Do" list gets so long you just have to throw it out and say, "I *To Did* nothing. Screw it."

Amy, a working mom of two, realized that her family members of the pet variety were just as much work as the others: "Those who know me know I love animals and have always had dogs. My first fur baby died when I was pregnant with my youngest. I was devastated, but soon it hit me that my life got easier in a sense without having to take care of him too. Then my second dog passed a couple years later and again relief came after the grief."

I can relate to Amy's feelings. We have two of the most annoying dogs on the planet and two cats who want nothing more than to be next to their person at all hours of the day. (Especially if the hour of the day is 3 AM.) My absolute favorite thing is waking up in the middle of the night to the sound of a cat coughing up a fur ball, or perhaps to a dog ass dangerously close to my nose.

I can't blame my animals for wanting to be close to me. Before I had kids they didn't have to compete for my attention, and now they have been moved to an unacceptably low priority. But sometimes adding in their meals and doctor's appointments and walks and poop and neediness can push me over the edge when it comes to calculating exactly how many lives I am responsible for on a daily basis.

Deanna, mom of three, constantly feels overwhelmed: "It can be so frustrating trying to be everybody's everything. My hope is that as my kids grow older they won't remember that I forgot little things or that I couldn't always juggle everything. Instead I hope they will remember how much they were loved."

Michelle is a stay-at-home mom who feels that she rarely gets a break: "Even when I try to go out without kids to try and have 'me time' I feel like I have to be home on time to get the kids in bed because bedtime goes more smoothly when I'm there. Ah! It's frustrating and so much pressure. Rewarding, yes. But frustrating."

Michelle echoes a lot of the other MOFL who feel that it's impossible to get a break. Our brains are constantly going over schedules and lists and dates, which means we never really have a moment to lay aside our responsibilities.

Monica, mom of four, has developed ways to deal with the stress in her life: "When I get overwhelmed or have something hanging over my head I do something that I like doing, like a craft or an art project that I've been putting off. That may seem like it would add more stress but somehow it doesn't. It shifts my focus; then after I'm done I'm ready to jump back into my crazy life again. I kinda get back into being 'me' again before I have to transform into my fake 'supermom/housekeeper/chef/chauffeur/ take care of everyone else's problems' role."

Monica touches on one of the most important things you can do to relieve the stress that comes from being responsible for so many others: remember that you are ultimately the only one responsible for yourself. Carving out ways to rejuvenate yourself may seem impossible, but it is in the best interest of everyone in your household. You are of no use to anyone if you are running on fumes.

Do things like setting up a sitter well in advance for a couple of date nights every month, and force yourself to go on those date nights even when it feels too difficult. Or maybe go see a movie alone. Or do anything alone, really. Reconnect with a hobby you used to love before you had kids. Read a book, watch a TV show, or sit in complete silence in a dark living room for half an hour after the kids are in bed.

- -

Also, if you have a partner, lean on them and delegate some of the responsibilities onto their plate. A lot of the time, moms take on everything and harbor resentment toward their partners for not helping out more. Sometimes they do this without even giving their partner the opportunity to help. So, although you are a control freak, go ahead and delegate a little. And if your partner messes it up, then you can harbor resentment for the right reasons.

Also, I hope all the stories told by my MOFL help you realize that you aren't the only one whose life isn't as easy as your Facebook posts make it out to be. Sometimes knowing that others are equally overwhelmed can help alleviate some of the pressure that we put on ourselves to keep up with unrealistic expectations.

It turns out we are all drowning, so at least you are in good company. Yay, camaraderie!

SO MUCH SPIRIT

- -

My mommy said it's crazy that she actually got my hair done at all given the crap morning we had.

My mommy said that California is in the west. So I'm wearing my swim suit under my clothes.

My mommy said I really like books that have strong female characters who wear pigtails. Then she said "Bam!"

CRAZY HAIR DAY   WESTERN DAY   DRESS LIKE YOUR
FAVORITE BOOK
CHARACTER DAY

- -

I'M NOT A big fan of the baby years. They are exhausting, confusing, and overall feel like some sort of endurance event that you haven't prepared yourself for on an emotional or physical level.

As my kids grew out of being babies, I started to feel a bit of relief. Regular sleep became a part of my life again (even though "regular" has become a very loose term after having children). The children started to communicate mostly (*mostly*) with words instead of bloodcurdling screams. And the days of living with people who pooped their pants while standing next to me were winding down. Oh, this was an exciting time indeed!

And then I let the children out into the world. That was an error in judgement. I highly recommend *not* doing this, if you can avoid it. Amazon and Netflix have plenty of educational shows to entertain your child at home. So there is really no reason to leave. Ever.

Because once you do allow the children to leave, they will be exiting your house and entering a world full of Spirit Days. Did you know that your kids can't learn anything without spirit getting involved? If you didn't know, you will find out soon enough.

It seems as though every school, daycare, gymnastics class, dance class, soccer class, music class, or drawing class is required by federal law to periodically schedule Spirit Days. And it won't take long for you to realize that Spirit Days have, ironically, been created to break yours.

Spirit Days are an attempt to make things more entertaining for children. Because we all know how lacking our children are in the fun department. I might point out that the school, daycare, and classes provide enough fun all on their own, but then I might be labeled a buzzkill. Because whatever would kids do if they didn't have Crazy Sock/Hair Day every couple of months? And is a childhood really a childhood if there aren't regularly scheduled reasons to wear a costume for the entire day?

As a working mom, I struggle with constantly feeling that my kids get the shaft because they are two of so many balls I'm juggling. To ease my guilt, I go out of my way to make sure that they are involved in plenty of activities. No, their mommy doesn't have the time (or the inclination, let's be honest) to do Pinterest-worthy arts and crafts, but at least they are enrolled in a class where they can learn how to do a somersault. And that's a skill that lasts so much longer than a craft, right?

I try not to overschedule the kids because they don't need constant entertainment. But just with preschool, gymnastics, and dance, I feel like we are always running late for something. (This is mostly due to the fact that we are always running late for something.)

Our mornings are spent battling to get the kids to eat something resembling breakfast and out the door wearing something resembling an appropriate outfit (matching shoes don't happen *every* day). I keep a calendar of the various events, activities, and birthday parties the kids have, and make sure they have the costumes, uniforms, and presents they need for each. My workday is cut short a couple of times a week so I can hustle a kid to one enriching class or another.

When we slide into said class forty-five seconds early, no one crying from our efforts to get there, I feel a brief sense of accomplishment. Pride, even. I'm pulling this off! Look at us! Balls juggled, bitches!

But then, just as Vivian scampers over to her gymnastics class, I realize that she's the only kid not wearing a Halloween costume. Her little face falls and takes my heart down with it.

Once again, we've been pummeled by a f'n Spirit Day.

That has happened more than once. I groan every time I see a note attached to Vivian's school bag, announcing some themed day that is happening that week. (Western Day? Really? Am I the only person who doesn't have western wear for my four-year-old at the ready?) Or when the dance class sends an email alerting me that it's Neon Day on Friday, or maybe Crazy Hair Day next week. You know what's crazy? That mommy even had time to brush her hair this morning before dance class. And you know what's impossible to do while wearing your elaborate princess Halloween costume? A f'n somersault.

It's hard not to feel that these Spirit Days are a direct attack on working parents, those of us who never quite have enough hours in the day to give our kids the time we think they deserve. Now we have to waste part of that limited time looking for a cowboy hat at Target on a Tuesday night. Or figuring out several different Halloween costumes because the holiday is now a month-long celebration that requires your kid to be in character for the entirety of October. When did everything get so damn precious?

Because my irritation level with Spirit Days fits with my overall disposition about the world in general, I thought I was probably alone in my hatred of all things theme-based. But when I started talking to other parents, I realized I am one of many dark souls who hate spirit.

Carrie, mom of two boys, feels my Western Day pain and raises me four more days: "For Halloween this year we have our costumes, but also this week is 'story character' week. Daily the kids dress like a favorite book character. Then Halloween on Friday. It's f'n nuts. I need five Halloween costumes instead of just one."

My aunt Deanna, a teacher for many years, is also not a fan of Spirit Days because they make teaching difficult: "Costume days at school cause a huge loss in instruction time! Kids can't/won't give their attention to the learning at hand when they are dressed in pajamas, have their hair in a crazy 'do, are in disguise as a character from a book, etc. I am all for a fun day once in a while, but there are more and more days dedicated to such things every year. Ask your school administrators to limit them!"

Maybe we could start a petition! But that sounds like it would take time. Foiled again!

For those of us with younger kids, Spirit Days are a small sampling of what is to come. Soon we will be buried in homework, sports, clubs, and socializing. How on earth are we going to have time for crazy hair?!

Dana, mom of two young kids, is terrified of what's in store: "My two kids are only in preschool. The oldest goes to dance one day a week now and sometimes that is a struggle. The poor second child isn't allowed an activity yet."

Jen's kids are older and fully immersed in the chaos: "Seriously! So many sports, activities, running around like a crazy person 24/7! I cleaned out my car the other day and I was mortified. We live in it! And let's not even start with the 356,886,543 birthday parties on the weekends while also playing three games on Saturday. This is why I drink wine!"

Sarah G., mom of four, can't figure out a free second for Children #3 and #4 to be involved in activities: "And that is why my third child has done nothing! I feel guilty all the time. But between the two older boys' school, homework, homework, homework, sports, and her kindergarten we have no time. And the fourth kid still poops his pants. And oh, yeah, I also have a job. I don't know when I could take her."

And please don't you dare utter the words *Elf on the Shelf* anywhere in the vicinity of a parent of small kids. Never has a symbol of holiday cheer created more homicidal urges.

"Mommy, everyone in my class has an Elf on the Shelf. Santa sends him to your house the month before Christmas if you are good, and the elf is in a different spot every morning when you wake up. Some elves even do fun stuff like bake cookies or ride on a rope swing from the chandelier down to the floor!"

"Oh, sweetie, I'm so glad that there is one more way for us to make Christmas magical for you! I just can't wait to see where that silly elf ends up every morning! Did you know that some of Santa's elves are really lazy and only move every five days or so? True story."

I recently noticed a commercial advertising *The Elf on the Shelf: A Birthday Tradition* because why stop at the month of December when I can just keep moving this elf around the house every night during the kid's birthday month too? I threw one of Vivian's western wear cowboy boots at the TV before she could catch sight of the commercial, narrowly escaping the pressure of any more spirit.

15

YOU NOW HAVE TO FEED TWO PEOPLE WHO REFUSE TO EAT

You're going to need a lot of chicken nuggets

WORLD'S WORST COOKING SHOW

I WILL BE THE first to point out that breastfeeding has its challenges (see Chapter 4: "Breastfeeding Is Still F'n Hard"). But what it lacks in overall ease, it makes up for in simplicity. Mealtime with a newborn isn't very complicated. Baby cries; baby gets boob or bottle. The end.

Things get a little less simple when you are breastfeeding Baby #2 because you are also responsible for the nourishment of a non-boob-fed child (think cutting an apple with a baby hanging off your nipple). But even that scenario is preferable to where you are eventually heading. Because once your body stops providing a majority of your second child's meals, you will be left dreaming of the days when losing an apple-holding finger was the worst thing that could happen during dinnertime.

As Baby #2 gets older, you find yourself in the most unfortunate of circumstances: feeding two children. Every damn day. And if you planned your children only a couple of years apart as I did, you will be blessed with feeding not only two children but two toddlers. If you aren't a praying person you might want to consider starting now, as you are going to need all the help you can get.

Contrary to popular and scientific belief, toddlers don't actually eat. At least not in any manner that resembles the eating habits of actual human people. And now you have two of them staring at you from across the table.

Children in general and toddlers specifically are demanding and picky. They can go for days at a time on only the three bites of food that accidently fly into their mouth instead of the floor during their mealtime toddler version of "Make it rain!" They can rarely be expected to entertain more than four different foods during a seven-day span, and what they lack in a mature *palate* they make up for in complete lack of acceptable table manners. They are an absolute delight to have at any table. And now they have taken over your table.

During this time you will be reintroduced to the delights of your youth. Chicken nuggets, tater tots, and PB&J sandwiches will dominate your menus, while homemade applesauce, vegetables made to look like cute faces, and food pyramids litter your Pinterest board. You have the best of intentions, but Mommy is tired and Easy Mac takes three minutes to prepare.

Now, some parents introduce "adult" foods to their children early and often and refuse to make separate meals for picky kids. Unfortunately for me, the only thing I did early and often with my children was Google "long-term effects of no sleep." The Easy Mealtime Ship sailed away quite a while ago (and left me on an island littered with hurled utensils and chicken nuggets).

For those of you who dread mealtimes as much as I do, I've prepared a step-by-step guide to feeding two picky kids during one mealtime. This guide includes handy recipes for two go-to meal options: peanut butter and jelly sandwiches and macaroni and cheese. These two meals may seem too simple for recipes, but cockiness like that has no place in child rearing.

HOW TO FEED TWO PICKY EATERS

INGREDIENTS NEEDED:

1 loaf of whole wheat bread (Whole wheat! Healthful!)
1 jar of peanut butter (Protein!)

1 jar of jelly (Fruit!)

1 box Kraft Mac and Cheese (Powdered cheese!)

3 tbsp milk (Dairy!)

3 tbsp butter (More dairy!)

1 box Kraft Easy Mac (Easy!)

1 bottle of wine (Fruit!)

It's dinnertime. The time of day when a family comes together around the table to enjoy a nice meal together and reflect on their day. Wait, that's an Olive Garden commercial. In reality, dinner can be the most stressful of times for parents whose children are picky eaters. You've had a long day, you're so close to bedtime that you can almost hear your pillow calling your name, and the sun may be even mocking you by setting long before anyone is going to be horizontal in your house. And then it's time to feed the children.

You've made a nice meal of steak and vegetable and maybe a potato. The children look at this meal as if you meant to put it in front of someone else. Because obviously that is not what they will be eating tonight. It's a bit amateurish that you even offered it, to be honest.

Child #1 would instead prefer a peanut butter and jelly sandwich, please. And no, Child #2 is not interested in one of those. Child #2 needs mac and cheese and for you to put a little hustle in your step. Neither one cares that your steak is getting cold. Stop being so self-centered.

Here are the easy steps you need to take to feed these children.

1. Bring a medium-size pot of water to a boil for Mac and Cheese.

2. Spread 1 tablespoon of peanut butter on one piece of bread.

3. Spread 1 tablespoon of jelly on another piece of bread.

4. Put pieces of bread together.

5. Cut sandwich in half.

6. Serve Child #1.

7. Start over when Child #1 has emotional breakdown because sandwich is cut in half.

8. Repeat steps 2–4.

9. Present sandwich to child.

10. Cut crusts off the sandwich per child's request/demand. (Note: Crusts are the devil's addition to all bread products.)

11. Present sandwich to child.

12. Confirm that the child actually wants you to cut the sandwich into a circle.

13. Confirm again.

14. Cut sandwich into a circle.

15. Present sandwich to child.

16. Cut circle sandwich into a star upon child's request.

17. Add macaroni to the boiling pot of water for Child #2.

18. Start over with your peanut butter and jelly project when Child #1 screams out to the heavens in protest of having only one star, when of course three stars are required because child is three years old (Note: Child was two years old when meal started).

19. Repeat steps 2–4, three times.

20. Cut out three star-shaped sandwiches.

21. Present sandwiches to child.

22. Start over when child discovers an extreme distaste for peanut butter.

23. Repeat steps 3–4, three times.

24. Cut out three star-shaped sandwiches.

25. Present sandwiches to child.

26. Discover the pot of water overflowing with foam, macaroni soggy.

27. Power forward despite near disintegration of macaroni.

28. Drain macaroni (if there is any water that hasn't been absorbed by the macaroni) and return blob to pot.

29. Add milk, butter, and cheese dust.

30. Stir gently in attempt to keep macaroni resembling anything close to macaroni.

31. Serve oatmeal-looking macaroni to Child #2.

32. Try to convince Child #1 that jelly dripping out of a sandwich is not akin to nuclear acid dripping out of sandwich and therefore a similar reaction is not required.

33. Carry Child #1 to sink and wash his or her hands and arms vigorously with soap and water to offset nuclear acid effects.

34. Start over with an Easy Mac when Child #2 refuses to eat your blob of Mac and Cheese.

35. Remove plastic cover from Easy Mac, open lid, fill cup with water to the noted "Fill Line," and place in the microwave for three minutes.

36. Give both children animal crackers (animal = protein!) and chewy fruit snacks (fruit!) for dinner.

37. Pour yourself a goblet of wine.

38. Find Easy Mac in microwave the next morning when heating up your coffee.

39. Think seriously about eating it.

16

YOU'LL HAVE A FAVORITE
Start saving for therapy now

THE WAY TO A MOM'S HEART

All that dog does all day is bark at the wind, chase squirrels he'll never catch, roll around in smelly things, try to get on my lap after rolling around in smelly things, and make poop deposits in the backyard that the kids will eventually step in and/or pick up with their hands. But he is the one living being in this house that doesn't wake me up at night. That makes him my favorite.

SNORE SNORE SNORE SNORE

*Y*OU'VE HEARD THE stories; you've read the inspirational quotes. You know that each time you bring home a new baby, your heart grows again and again. As a parent you will always have enough love to go around. You could never pick a favorite, that's for sure!

Except that is a load of crap. Of course you'll have favorites. You know how I know this to be true? Because your children are actually just little people (despite the fact that their poor manners and lack of effective communication skills leave them more closely resembling monkeys). And people, no matter how cute their pigtails or how innocent their smiles, are all assholes at least some of the time. It's just science. In fact, children are assholes more often than your average human (with their poor manners and lack of effective communication skills). And assholes start moving down the favorite list pretty quickly.

The only difference between your kid and any other asshole is you can't actually admit that your kid's behavior is making you like them less. If you admit it, then all of a sudden *you're* the asshole.

On a Saturday morning (which used to be the time of the week I spent facedown in a pillow) when sweet Daniel is wide awake at 6 AM while his beautiful sister sleeps until 8:30 AM, I have been known to say, "My *favorite* child is still sleeping." Or perhaps, "My favorite child slept all night last night!" (Please note that my love is entirely dependent on how much sleep you allow me.) Then any other adult in the vicinity will gasp, "Don't say that!"

Why? It's just a little joke. Or is it? (It's not.)

There will be moments when each child will make your heart soar with love. And other moments when they make you want to lock yourself in the pantry for three hours (that's where all the wine and snacks are hidden). Some kids are heavy on the heart-soaring, and others inspire a deadbolt on the pantry door. ("Mommy is on time-out! She'll come out when you are thirty-three years old!")

It doesn't mean you "love" the children any less, but sometimes they do make it difficult to "like" them a whole hell of a lot.

When I asked my MOFL about having favorites, I wasn't sure they would admit to their real feelings. But once again, they had no problem telling the truth. And also no problem acknowledging that we are all going to hell for these truths.

In talking with my MOFL about favorites, the word *easy* came up a lot. As in, whoever is being the easiest tends to move quickly into the top spot on Mommy's list. One mom said, "The amount of love I have for them is the same; one is just 'easier' to love. If that makes sense?"

Yes, it makes perfect sense to anyone who has spent their days ramming their head against the will of a person who may be tiny in stature but is overflowing with stubborn. Kaysee, mom of three, says this in a slightly more tactful way: "I can't imagine life without any of them, but different personalities are definitely easier to get along with!"

Recently I attended an out-of-town wedding with my parents and Vivian. The wedding took place five hours away. While planning the trip, I decided almost immediately that Daniel would not be coming along for the ride. First of all, strapping him in a car for five hours sounded like a form of medieval torture for him and every other passenger's eardrums. Second, Daniel is not really known for his consistent behavior in public. Taking him to a wedding or reception seemed like a surefire way to bring both of those gatherings to a screeching (literally) halt.

A couple of days before we were scheduled to leave on our trip, Becky texted me: "Maybe you could take Daniel with you, so I can get some work done this weekend."

To which I responded, "HAAAAAAAAAAAAAAAAAAAAA AAAAAAAAAAAAAAAAAAAAAAAAAAAAAAAAAAAAAAAAA AAAAAAAAAAAAAAAAAAAAAAAAAAAAAAAAAAAAAAAAA AAAAAAAAAAAAAAAAAAAAAAAAAAAAAAAAAAAAAAAAA AAAAAAAAAAAAAAAAAAAAAAAAAAAAAAAAAAAAAAAAA AAAAAAA." And that was the end of the texting conversation.

Look, I love the kid with all my heart. But he's a toddler in every sense of the word. He screams when he's happy, sad, frustrated, or tired. He has a (randomly set) internal timer that goes off at some point during every meal that tells his brain that it is now time to stand up in his chair and throw his food across the room. He poops his pants. And him sleeping in any bed that isn't his own usually results in little to no actual sleeping for anyone within a one-mile radius.

So, yeah, he wasn't going on the road trip.

Vivi, by contrast, has two years on her brother, and she has always been a really "easy" kid. She patiently rode in the car for five hours and quietly sat through all of our meals on the road. She was well-behaved and polite at the wedding and kept herself entertained, even when I knew she was bored out of her mind. She was easy.

Michaela, mom of a toddler boy and an infant girl, reports a similar dynamic: "I have one that's easier than the other. Sam, I love him so much, but he's very independent and strong-willed and not a snuggle bug at all. I'm always trying to navigate his willfulness and determination. Whereas the baby is so happy and easy. So, I don't have a favorite, but Sam gets about a million times more of my energy and attention than sweet Nora."

Debbie, mom of five, started out with two very reserved boys. Then she added three girls to the mix, and all hell broke loose. "When these crazy little girls came along, it was an adjustment. Grace was a little nuts but good. Aubrey was pretty relaxed and sweeter, so I cuddled with her more, and I just felt like we just had a deeper connection. But then came Brynn. She was the best form of birth control out there. I always wondered what I did so wrong. She's getting better now and she's far more cuddly than she used to be, but it was hard sometimes not to feel like she was my punishment for something. And yes, I'm going to hell . . ."

Debbie mentioned something a lot of the other moms noted, that we tend to feel closer to the kids who snuggle the most. To the ones who want to be closer to us. In my case I still say yes when Daniel asks me to rock him to sleep at night. He's way too big and he shouldn't need to be held, but I so enjoy those moments with him snuggled up against me, quiet and peaceful. I usually hold him long after he's fallen asleep, using that time to reset my love for him after a day navigating his antics.

I'm grateful that I still have those moments with Daniel because it can be hard to connect with a kid when you can never slow him down long enough for a hug or a quick kiss. Sometimes it feels like we are holding on tight and they are just getting further and further away, with some kids moving quicker than others.

Deanna, mom of three, admits that she feels closer to the child who needs her more: "I love all of my kids with my whole heart. But, my son has a different grip on my heart than my girls do. I think it might be because they are both so independent. Which I love, but it makes me sad at the same time. He tends to need me more, which I love!" Except for when she needs some pantry time: "Until I want him to do something independently; then it is a whole other story."

And that's the thing. The favorite isn't set in stone; it's usually just the kid who is the smallest pain in your ass at any given moment. Michelle, mom of two, has a constantly changing front-runner: "My 'favorite' switches from hour to hour, sometimes minute to minute. Whoever is sleeping or behaving at the moment wins out."

Sarah G., mom of four, admits to shifting loyalties as well: "I totally have favorites. And they rotate depending on their season. Jake is the kindest, most polite, and most hardworking kid ever; he makes my heart swell with pride. Until he acts like a butthole and then I can't stand him. Theo is super-rad, fiercely independent, and really funny. Until his independence means he's not listening to me; then I want to punch him. Bea is such a GIRL and I love it!!!! Then she's a girl and she drives me insane. Louie is awesome, all the time. There, I said it: the baby really is the favorite! Ha!"

Don't worry too much or beat yourself up if you end up having a favorite now and then. Kids are nothing if not constantly changing creatures. In my case, I assume Daniel's monkey-like antics will seem charming compared to the wonders that Vivian will have in store for me during her emotional teen years (she might lock herself in the pantry during that time). And even now, in between his tantrums and throwing of food, Daniel always stops me each day, grabs my face, and gives me a kiss on each cheek for no apparent reason. I think he knows it's my favorite.

THE SH!T NO ONE TELLS YOU

Journal Entry

MY LITTLE BOY IN PINK BOOTS

Daniel's early toddler years were marked by a lot of screaming, crying, falling, and throwing of food. It was almost as if his brain was alerted at age twelve months and one day that it was officially time to kick things up a notch. No more peaceful adorableness would be tolerated; it was time to start making a mark on the world. And on his forehead. And my kitchen floor.

It's not as if this behavior was unexpected; he is far from the first child to embrace the Wrath of the Toddler. But there was one thing he added to his repertoire that I wasn't quite expecting: accessories. And, my good lord, does this child know how to put an outfit together.

Like many other kids, he started off simply enough, by putting anything on his head that would fit. Boxes, Tupperware, underwear, bras—anything within reach would promptly be tried on as headwear. That was adorable, of course, but it was just a taste of what was in store.

As he got bigger Daniel moved on to other accessories: shoes, ties, necklaces, shoes, costumes, jackets, and also some shoes. He really enjoyed shoes. It got to the point at which the question "Where is Daniel?" could always by answered by "In the shoe closet." And there you would find him, sitting on a pile of shoes, debating which ones to put on (rarely did he go with a matching pair).

More often than not he would pick his sister's shoes, mostly because they were big enough for him to get on without having

---

to ask for help. And then around the corner my boy would come stomping, wearing a backpack, sunglasses, hard hat, and his sister's pink snow boots. In the middle of summer.

When he first started accessorizing, I thought it was hilarious. Seeing him load various items onto his body was endlessly entertaining. And more than that, it seemed to entertain him. Any activity that kept him happy and tantrum-free for a few minutes was always a welcome addition to the day.

Then he started wanting to go out of the house dressed in whatever mismatched outfit he had assembled. And I hesitated. I'm not sure why, exactly. Well, that's not true; I am sure why. I was embarrassed. But why was I embarrassed? He was two years old, and clearly happy as a clam to be wearing his socks on his hands and his sister's huge pink necklace around his neck.

I'm a relatively quiet person, and I really don't enjoy standing out in the crowd. I was the kid who always sat in the back of the class and prayed, prayed, prayed that I wouldn't be called upon. Taking a kid out and about who looked noticeably different than a "normal" kid made me feel uncomfortable. Because we certainly weren't going to be blending in.

But out we went. Because it made the boy happy, and I'm not in the habit of picking unnecessary fights with Tyrant Toddlers.

No, we didn't blend in, but Daniel didn't seem to care much. There stomped my boy, wearing his sister's pink boots, or his Spider-Man mask, or his shirt on backward and inside out because he insisted on dressing himself. He didn't really understand why people would look at him and say, "Hey, there, little man!" or why other kids would be drawn to the various parts of his ensemble. In his mind there was nothing weird about what he was wearing because they were all just things he was drawn to on that particular day. Judging by people's reactions to Daniel's appearance, I think we are all a little nostalgic for that brief time in our lives when we honestly don't give a shit what anyone else thinks.

I often wonder if this aspect of his personality will stick with him through the years. Will I be seeing pictures of my twenty-one-year-old son at a party dressed in whatever ridiculous costume college kids find amusing (I'm assuming the underwear being worn inappropriately will make a comeback around that age)? God, I hope so.

Over time I've stopped being embarrassed about Daniel's outfits and started to embrace them for what they are: a delightful manifestation of a little kid's imagination. I love that he is still at the age where the only thing guiding his decisions is what makes him feel good. And I'm hoping that by embracing his "weird" fashion sense we are, in some small way, teaching him that he's not weird at all.

Someday the world may tell him something different, and when that happens I hope he still puts on those zebra sunglasses, pulls down his Ninja Turtle helmet, adjusts his pretty necklace, and lets the world know that they are missing out on a ton of fun. Walk tall, my little man in pink boots. Walk tall.

A BLOSSOMING RELATIONSHIP

*P*LEASE TURN BACK to the front of this book, to the dedication page. Do you see that adorable photo of my two babies "meeting" each other? Isn't it the cutest thing you've ever seen? I found a picture similar to that on Pinterest when I was pregnant with Daniel, and I stored it in my mind as the perfect representation of sibling love.

The fact that Vivian had to be bribed with fruit snacks to even stand in that doorway for the photo is a good example of how sibling relationships actually unfold. I have an outtake from that photo session in which my firstborn is standing on the threshold, arms crossed, frown firmly planted on her face, seemingly guarding the house from this intruder. That picture more accurately represents the underlying emotions she was feeling when Daniel arrived.

A lot of us go into the multiple children game with deceptive professional photography as our inspiration. Look how cute the Williams boys are on their Christmas card! All color-coordinated and smiley! Oh my goodness, the Smith kids always look so angelic in the photos they post on Facebook twice a year! They are in nature; they are embracing; they are a delight!

Then you have two children of your own and you instantly want to file a lawsuit against the Williams and Smith families for false advertising. You were expecting your household to look like a Norman Rockwell painting and instead you are stuck in a Jackson Pollock disaster.

Although, to be fair, you can't actually blame it on the Williams and Smith families. The real descent from adorable to deplorable in your house can usually be directly tied to That Damn Toy. Without That Damn Toy, everything would be fine.

You may wonder what toy I'm referring to exactly, so you can avoid buying it yourself. But the great thing about That Damn Toy is that it can be Any Damn Toy. And really, it doesn't even need to be a toy at all. Anything that will fit into the hands of or can just be touched by a child is potentially the object that will bring everything crashing down.

At any given moment, your house can be brought to its knees when both children decide they want the same toy. It doesn't matter if they are sitting in a playroom that looks like it's just been bombed by Toys 'R Us. Both of them need to have That One Damn Toy. They cannot imagine their lives without it. But they can imagine your life if they don't get it, and that life is not going to be a peaceful one.

Almost all the sibling squabbles in our house can be traced back to toys. One child (Child A) has a toy, while the other child (Child B) is playing quietly in another part of the room/house/time zone. Then Child B looks up from her quiet play, and something deep inside her sets off an alarm that it is time for action. Quick, noisy, and destructive action. Her head snaps in the direction of Child A. She locks her focus on the toy in Child A's hands. She gets up, scurries across the room—tripping over piles of other, probably better, toys—and lunges at That Damn Toy in Child A's hands. The toy must be Child B's; the universe demands it.

Several things will happen at this point, ranging from fighting to crying to Mommy searching Expedia for the next available flight out of the country. Child A will hold on fiercely to That Damn Toy. Even though he has only been playing with it for five minutes, it's his most favorite toy he has ever encountered.

Child B is appalled that the toy is not handed over upon demand. Perhaps a louder demand is required to speed up this transaction. Mommy tries desperately to point out the other toys available. But no one is interested in her point of view.

The playroom is quickly transformed into a UFC octagon when both children deem That Damn Toy to be worthy of a fight to the death. Hair will be pulled, less attractive toys will be hurled, and bodies will be tackled. As Mommy breaks up the brawl, she will wonder why all the adorable sibling photos on Pinterest didn't come with warning labels.

Just as Mommy is ready to set fire to the playroom to avoid any future squabbles, Child A nonchalantly drops That Damn Toy and shifts his focus to something different. Child B runs to That Damn Toy, clutching it like a lost puppy that has been found. Everything is right in the world.

Fourteen seconds later, Child B loses interest in That Damn Toy and goes to a different part of the room to play quietly. As if no lives (or mental stabilities) were in danger mere minutes prior.

Mommy pours a glass of wine and huddles in the corner, knowing it's just a matter of time until another Damn Toy comes along to wreak havoc on all within its view.

It has become very clear why all those professional photos of children are taken outside. It's an effort to get the siblings as far away from toys as possible.

Moms on the Front Lines

SHARING

There are various opinions on teaching kids to share. For a long time, it was standard practice to force kids to share in all situations and circumstances. Why? Because kids are innately self-centered beings, and sharing would make them acknowledge that there are other people in the world. Sharing would also build them into compassionate individuals who would grow up to be kind and generous to their fellow humans, so said science.

But then science realized that forcing children to automatically share everything with everyone who ever demanded it wasn't preparing them for life so much as it was teaching them how to get walked all over. It was also teaching kids that anything could be theirs at any moment they chose. It didn't matter how the other kids felt; it was time to share, dammit! You see how science might have not totally thought this through.

These days, opinions about sharing have been shifting. More and more parents refuse to teach their kids to share simply because another child demands it. This change is being implemented in schoolyards and also in homes. Kids are still encouraged to share and take turns, but now a toy is only up for grabs when a child is done playing with it. A lesson in delayed gratification never hurt anyone (unless you are counting the eardrums of the adult who has to listen to a toddler demand a toy be his).

In my house, we don't force the kids to share with their sibling. If the toy is appropriate for sharing, such as blocks or a pile of cars, then we ask the kids to share and allow the child who is playing with the toys to pick a few to share with his sibling. If the toy is not sharable, then we ask the child using the toy to please give it to his sibling when he is done playing. That works a lot of the time, but sometimes the child demanding the toy has an epic meltdown because her wishes have been denied. Even in this case, we still don't force the child with the toy to share. This is always fun and makes playtime simply magical.

I asked my MOFL about sharing rules in their households. They too struggle with children who can't quite grasp the concept.

Jen has come up with a perfect way to avoid fighting: "I try to avoid my kids having to share with each other! They each get the exact same thing."

I too have resigned myself to the fact that the only real way to ensure peace in my house is to buy two of everything for the next fifteen years or so. It's not great for my budget, but it's a plan concocted primarily for the sake of my sanity.

It is always necessary to get them not only an equal number of items or toys but also *exactly* the same items or toys. Every time we get Happy Meals, I ask for two meals with the exact same toy, a concept not easily grasped by fast-food employees. They don't seem to understand the grave consequences to the mental well-being of my entire family if the toys are not *exactly* the same.

"I asked for two of the same toy."

"Those are two ponies."

"The ponies are different colors! One color is clearly superior!! I need matching colors!!"

So you see, the plan is going really well so far.

162 THE SH!T NO ONE TELLS YOU

Jill tries to keep calm in her house by putting off the sharing: "We have always told our kids that if they want something to let the other person know by saying, 'When you are done playing with that, I would like it.'"

We do that as well, and it always baffles me that Daniel usually calms down when it is promised that he'll get the toy after Vivian is done with it. Since there are only two children in the house, I'm not sure who exactly he thinks is next in line for the toy, but logical thought processing has never been his strong suit.

Sarah B. has several sharing rules: "If they can't agree on how to share it, I usually take the toy away. If one clearly had it first, they get to keep it. If the other one wants it, I set a timer. It would be nice if they would share. But that rarely happens."

If our kids get to a toy at the same time and can't figure out how to share it, then the toy is taken away. And a chorus of crying is cued. On occasion, this crying has snapped the brain of one of the adults in our house, and a few toys may have been sawed in half during such incidents. FYI: This solution just causes more crying (of the horrified variety), so you probably don't want to try it in your own home.

Jen has come up with some ways to make sharing easier: "Sometimes they have to share, for instance, when there is only one brownie left. In that case one cuts it and the other chooses the piece they want first. I also have marble jars at my house (they each have their own jar, of course). When that marble jar is full they get to choose something they want to do or a special prize. I give marbles for kindness, sharing, making good choices, etc. So that helps."

When all else fails, a little bribery never hurt anyone.

Amy tries to encourage her kids to share: "We always stress the manners/politeness side of it. It's true you don't have to share, but it's nice to share. We focus on that aspect."

Most often I find myself teaching that lesson when Vivian and Daniel are interacting with other kids. No, you never *have* to share, but it is nice to be generous with other people. I stress that most with respect to guests that come to our house. Kids, probably because they have control over so little in their lives, can sometimes hold on a little too tight to anything they deem "theirs." I try to teach them that it can actually be a lot of fun to share with other people, especially things that we really like ourselves.

As they get older, kids start to understand that sharing doesn't mean you are giving the toy away forever; it just means you are letting someone else have fun playing with it for a little while. Daniel, in all his toddler glory, doesn't particularly like either of these options and still holds on to everything as though it is going to be thrown into an incinerator the second he allows it to leave his arms.

So you see, my plan is going really well so far.

MOM'S BRAIN IS A COMPLEX PLACE

our turn to bring snacks to soccer • get presents for birthday parties • 4 parties this weekend • vet appt. • WINE • kid's haircut • shave it all off • sign up jenny for swim lessons • buy jenny a swimsuit • buy a muumuu for me • kids' doctor appt. • kids' dentist appt. • kids' vision appt. • grocery shopping • healthy food • stuff my kids will actually eat • pantry snacks for me • only brown food for mikey • WINE • dance recital • pay for costume, pictures, flowers, commemorative video • schedule: bug guy, phone guy, gutter guy • clean: dishes, laundry, car, purse, cat box, dog run, desk, living room, children • WINE

I can't remember why I came into this room . . .

*T*HE OTHER DAY I was cleaning out the pantry and I found the certificate we got at the hospital when Vivian was born, the one that has her statistics and her little footprints. We had been storing it next to the chicken noodle soup, as you do. Earlier in the week I'd found a lock of hair from Daniel's first haircut. It was in a Ziploc baggie that had "Daniel's First Haircut" written on it with a Sharpie. It was in the deep fryer in the back of a kitchen cabinet.

GOOD NEWS: We don't deep-fry that often.

BAD NEWS: All my kids' childhood memories seem to be hidden in the kitchen for some reason.

When Vivian came along, I had high hopes of documenting her milestones in an adorable baby book that she would one day skim through while noting what detail-oriented parents she had. The fact that her baby book is completely empty five years after her birth means that she will just have to rummage through our cabinets if she wants more information.

By the time Daniel came along, I was not better at keeping track of details, but I had realized my limitations. I knew I wasn't going to sit down and note every milestone in a baby book. One, I have horrible handwriting that would make his milestones impossible to read. And two, my memory is not big on retaining information for longer than about twelve seconds.

But I really wanted my kids to have something they could look at when they were older. A book, an album—something that had details that none of our brains would remember otherwise. The tiny moments that make up a childhood—not just the major milestones.

I've come up with several ways to do this over the years. I will impart them to you now so that your kids can have their childhood memories housed somewhere besides your brain. Because we all know that storage device has an error message blinking most of the time. And the software will have expired long before your kids are grown.

SOCIAL MEDIA BOOKS

I realized early on that although I couldn't seem to find the time to jot down two words in a baby book, I had no problem documenting my children's every bowel movement on social media (sorry about that, social media). Most people would not consider that to be the best habit, but at least I was recording it somewhere.

I did a search and found several sites that allow you to print books of your social media posts. And all of a sudden, I had very detailed baby books.

Every year I print my Facebook feed as a yearbook for the kids. Not all of my posts are about them, but I figure my other posts will be an interesting time capsule of sorts for them someday: "Look at all those recipes she posted and never actually cooked!" And of course, "She sure thought cat memes were funny."

Now that I know I'm printing my time line, I make a point to post pictures of the kids' major events and the funny stuff they are into at any given time. Sometimes I post the pictures so that only I can see them, to make sure they end up in the book but not on everyone else's feed. Another cool feature of some of these books is that they also print out the comments on each post. So someday the kids can see what their grandparents and other relatives posted years before.

Sure, my kids may look at these books and wonder why I wasn't able to print out actual photo albums yet seemed to have ample time to peruse social media. But hopefully the hilarious cat memes will distract them from dwelling on that fact for too long.

A-LINE-A-DAY JOURNAL

I found little journals called "A Line a Day" that have a date at the top of every page. Then beneath that date, they have room for five years' worth of entries. Each night we write one or two lines about that day. When the book is done, we'll have a five-year journal with one or two sentences written every day. We can flip to the page for June 23 and see what happened on that date for five years in a row.

It might seem overwhelming to write in a journal that often, but it's only a couple of lines, which are really easy to get down right before you face-plant into bed. Then you and your kids have a crazy-detailed yet ultimately simple journal of your lives. It's great because they don't remember all the little things and you forget absolutely everything five seconds after your head hits the pillow.

TICKET ALBUM

I have an album for each kid that is made specifically for tickets. I put tickets in there as we go to different movies, shows, the circus, or their recitals. I'm a bit of a hoarder, and I love finding old tickets and playbills in my boxes of stuff from years' past. Essentially, this is a little more organized way to hoard.

EMAIL ADDRESSES

I don't use this one as much as I should, but I've set up an email address for both Vivian and Daniel. Periodically, I'll forward emails to their addresses or write them an email to tell them something I think may be interesting to read in twenty years. I've encouraged their grandparents to do the same. I love the idea of them having an inbox full of messages when they are older. As well as some fantastic deals on pharmaceuticals, I assume.

ONE DAMN PHOTO ALBUM

I have one photo album for each kid that I'm filling with only a few photos from each year. I put in any major holiday photos (crying with Easter Bunny, crying with Santa, frowning while I try to get a picture of both of them in their Halloween costumes, etc.), invitations to their birthday parties, our family Christmas card, and any official school, dance, or sports photos. I figure these pictures cover most of the highlights of the year, and if they want more information they are welcome to explore the 400,000 photos I've taken each year that are stored on my hard drive.

ALL THESE IDEAS are attempts to share my kids' childhoods with them in different ways. These various memory-keeping devices are just as much for me as they are for Vivian and Daniel. Life can become a bit of a blur when you spend it corralling kids each day. Reading back through their Line-a-Day books or my social media posts reminds me of so many little things I've already forgotten. And I hope someday all those books and albums can give the kids a glimpse not only into their childhoods but also into how incredibly loved they were every day of their lives. Most important, I'd like them to get a very clear idea of how little sleep they were allowing us. Because it's never too early to start thinking about how to guilt-trip your adult children.

Journal Entry

TRADITION! TRADITION!

It's important for children to have traditions in their lives, moments they can look back on and use to fondly piece together a memory collage of a magical childhood. Okay, "magical" might be pushing it, but I'm hoping that my Photoshop skills can leave a doctored photo trail of perfection, even if we were never quite able to hit that mark in real life.

During the holidays, the magic is turned up a few notches, and it's vitally important to maximize all the wonder you can by establishing family traditions early and often. One holiday tradition we've observed with the kids each year is to go on an adventure to cut down our Christmas tree. We venture out into nature, hack away at nature, and mount nature in our living room for a month. So magical.

The first Christmas with Daniel, we made it only as far as a weird farm down the street that randomly grew Christmas trees.

Not really magical, but convenient, which in itself is magical when you have a six-month-old baby.

The second year, we went to our normal spot up in the mountains about an hour away. Daniel cried the entire drive and fell 859 times while we hiked, and Becky ended up with a fat lip from the tree massacre. It was light on magic and heavy on head injuries.

I had high hopes for Daniel's third trip. He was much more coordinated, Vivian was excited, and, most important, we had recently purchased a car with a DVD player in it. That would go a long way toward making the drive more bearable for all involved.

Unfortunately, the DVD player stopped working before we even got to the freeway. Daniel found this development to be less than magical. He immediately commenced his holiday screaming, which is the most consistent holiday tradition we'd made to date.

I found a holiday station on the radio and was able to distract the kids for half of the ride with "Jingle Bells" and "Frosty" ditties.

Then we experienced our first holiday miracle when the movie player magically started playing. Daniel once again believed in Christmas. Vivian, however, was devastated that our caroling was coming to an end and insisted that the holiday songs stay on. Daniel insisted that we watch the movie that he had seen 942 times. Each child was moved to tears.

I was able to accommodate both children by somehow playing the movie on the screen and the radio station on the speakers. Daniel didn't seem to care that his movie had become a musical. That probably doesn't bode well for his future intelligence, but for one moment in time it was great.

➤

When we got up to the nature, there was snow on the ground. Our California kids had never actually been in snow before and were ecstatic. Then they discovered that snow is very cold. The kids were less excited about that fact.

We piled the shivering children into the bed of a rickety old 1940s pickup truck so we could maximize the holiday experience by being driven farther up into the nature. I was the last person to climb in, and I held Vivian on my lap. It turns out the holiday experience didn't involve a lot of safety precautions because, to my horror, this truck didn't actually have a tailgate that closed to hold all of the nature-seekers in the bed as it lurched up a 90-degree incline. Becky held on to me, and I held on to Vivian as I thought about how non-life-threatening it is to buy a tree from a grocery store parking lot.

We experienced our second miracle of the day by surviving the treacherous trip up the mountain. But when we got up there, we found that the recent drought had left very few trees. We hiked all around, the children periodically crashing to the ground when they slid on the slick snow. They were devastated to discover that snow is not actually big piles of cotton as they had always imagined. Instead, it was big piles of wet. Our magic was dwindling as their pants got wetter and wetter.

We searched and searched and searched for the tree that would give its life for our holiday cheer, but all the trees were less than merry. After nearly losing Daniel off a couple of steep cliffs, I headed back toward the drop-off point to look around. When I got there, I noticed a bunch of nice trees propped up against a fence. They had tags on them that read PRE-CUT.

Becky herded the children toward me, and I pointed to a beautiful, already chopped tree. Frozen, wet, and tired, she shrugged and said, "Sure."

When we got the merry tree back down the hill, it was the envy of everyone in the checkout line. We told them that it was pre-cut, probably from a little farther up in the nature. Our superiority was shattered when one of the employees chimed in with, "Those pre-cut trees came from Oregon. We didn't have enough of our own because of the drought."

So let us review. We drove one hour through screams and tears up to the frozen wilderness, risked our lives in the back of a rickety truck, developed frostbite by hiking in the snow for half an hour, and ultimately bought a tree that was from an entirely different state. The same tree that they have in the grocery store parking lot.

God bless us, every one.

The previous year we were able to fit our tree in the back of the SUV, and our newer SUV was even bigger, so we figured we'd have no problem fitting the tree inside this year as well. Unfortunately, Oregon grows very large trees, so we were forced to tie the tree to the top of the car. The nature people were nice enough to give us a hand and some string, and we headed off toward home.

I kept an eye on the tree through the sunroof as Becky drove down the freeway. I was also responsible for keeping an eye on the children and preparing a light afternoon snack to replenish all those hiking calories. After handing the kids their snacks, I looked up to the roof of the car to check on the tree. The tree wasn't there.

➤

"The tree is gone!" I yelled and motioned to the side of the road. Becky pulled over.

I looked behind us on the freeway to see if our wayward tree was causing a twenty-five-car holiday pile-up. Thankfully, it was not. I shifted in my seat to look at the roof of the car, and I could see that the tree was hanging off the side.

We re-centered the tree and decided that the only way to keep it on the car for the rest of the trip was to hold on to it. So we opened the sunroof and in freezing temperatures, going 70 miles per hour on the freeway, we switched off holding our tree on the last leg of its long trek from Oregon.

Another year of our magical holiday tradition concluded with frozen hands and two children complaining that the sunroof noise was drowning out their movie. Fa la la friggin' la.

PEOPLE WHO KEEP HAVING KIDS JUST REALLY HATE SLEEP

19

Or themselves. Or both.

JUST SLEEP WHEN THE KIDS SLEEP

*a*s an only child who came from a pretty tiny extended family, I had dreams of having a big family of my own someday. Because, as you know, the grass is always greener. Then I had two kids, and I realized that the grass was actually just a lot louder (see Chapter 12: "Everything Is So Damn Loud").

This noise overloaded my little brain, which was accustomed to an abundance of quiet. Suddenly, it became quite clear that I (or at least my brain) just wasn't cut out for a houseful of kids.

When I see people with a gaggle of children, it's like looking at an advanced physics equation. I just can't compute how it is possible. When do these people sleep? How do their refrigerators hold enough food to feed all those growing bodies? And most pressing of all, do they ever accidently forget to load one into the car?

Another aspect of having a lot of children that seems daunting is the fact that you are constantly starting over. Some people find this exciting because, for reasons I don't totally understand, they love babies. In my mind, the thought of starting over with a new blob every couple of years sounds like participating in a grueling endurance event that keeps moving the finish line. (It's also an endurance event in which my body gets worse and worse as the miles wear on.)

When we were struggling through the various ups and downs of Vivian's first couple of years, there was always a little voice in the back of my head reminding me that I would be traveling down this bumpy road again someday. It was an extra weight that I carried around.

These days I do a moderate to long celebratory dance each time we get past a difficult hurdle with Daniel. See ya later, baby years! I may stage a ceremonial burning of the diaper pail when (if?) he ever gets potty-trained. I'm not sure my fragile psyche could take the thought of starting over at day one with another baby. And I'm not sure the charred diaper pail would complement a new nursery.

My general confusion over why anyone would want a bunch of kids is a direct result of how I was raised. I was the only kid and also one of the calmest children ever recorded in nature. So our house was an extremely quiet one. When my kids have their friends over and the house is bursting with children and their accompanying noise, my heart starts racing with anxiety. Is there a volume button somewhere?

When I reached out to my MOFL about the number of children they wanted, they reported that the number of siblings they had also played a big role in their decisions.

Both Sarah B. and her husband came from families of two children, and they stopped after having two kids of their own: "We always said two. I surprised myself after Owen by really wanting a third. I'm glad now that we stopped at two. We have what we can handle!"

Sarah G. had four siblings growing up: "I always wanted four or five. Then after our third, we thought we decided we were done. Then God gave us four anyway and I couldn't be happier!!! Lucky Louie is my daily reminder that God has bigger plans for your life than you can dream of or plan for! I love the noise and chaos of my household, LOVE it. I miss my kids all day long, I'm sad dropping them off at school. I wish I could put them all back in my belly so we could go everywhere together. I come from a big family and got married at twenty-one years old, so I really don't know any other way of life!"

Michelle and her husband had a difference of opinion: "I come from a family of four, so growing up I always said I wanted four. My husband comes from a family of two, so he always said he wanted no more than two. One drunken pre-marriage night he agreed to three. He now denies this. So we have two. I would still love to have a third."

Amy thinks two is her max: "I felt I always wanted two. I wanted man-to-man defense. But when I had problems getting pregnant with one, I felt lucky to even have her. When we decided to try for the second, we didn't have our hopes up and said we'd give it a year, then call it quits. Well, I got pregnant, and when I had my first checkup I asked the doctor when was too soon for my husband to have a vasectomy and made sure she knew I wanted my tubes tied if I needed a C-section. (She told me to calm down and to get through the delivery first!)"

Leah originally wanted four kids, but then they started popping out a little too quickly: "For us the spacing was a large determining factor. When the third came sooner than intended, I thought I'd die if we had a fourth close enough to keep them all spaced out the same amount of years. That would have made four under five years old. So we called it quits. We didn't want there to be a straggler who felt left out."

Michaela is tempted to have more kids because she is still a little loopy from the sleep deprivation of having two kids: "I think we were always going to stop after two no matter the gender. Immediately after having our second, I felt a hard 'no way would I EVER have a third.' But, now I'm like, 'A third would be so fun (for the kids).'"

I'm not sure exactly why the unique mixture of sleep deprivation and poor hygiene of parenthood often leads people to believe that having more kids is a good idea. You must be strong and fight these urges. Don't look at baby pictures and *Oooo* and *Ahhhh* over how tiny and nonverbal your kids once were. Don't go through the boxes of their old clothes and start rewriting history about what your life was like when they fit into those tiny outfits. That is very dangerous. Don't conjure up memories about how they felt and smelled when they were brand-new. Don't do it!

You're doing it, aren't you?

Dammit.

Time to go buy a new diaper pail.

20

HAVING KIDS LOOKS A LOT EASIER ON TV

Because on TV they are never actually around

KIDS ARE THE BIGGEST DIVAS

Child labor laws only allow kids to work a few hours a day on a television show because that's as long as anyone can stand them.

I GREW UP WATCHING a lot of TV. This was before mommy blogs, so no one saw anything wrong with the fact that all my time was screen time. And now I can tell you that science is right on this one: TV really is bad for you. But not for all the reasons that the mommy blogs spout.

I don't have ADHD or diminished intelligence because of watching TV. But what I do have is even worse: I have very unrealistic expectations for what it means to have kids. TV, with your attractive parents, children who are offscreen most of the time, and problems that are solvable in thirty minutes or less, you have led me down a very dangerous path. A path that had me expecting parenting to come with a laugh track. (Okay, so maybe my intelligence is a little diminished . . .)

It turns out parenting in real life is nothing like parenting on most television shows. But there are some shows worth watching if you want a better idea of what it means to have kids. If you are looking for real educational programming, I have some viewing suggestions for you.

WHAT YOU THOUGHT PARENTING WAS GOING TO BE LIKE: *FULL HOUSE*

Look how well those three guys are raising those girls! They don't know much about parenting, but they are knocking it out of the park! They are full of sensitive advice, and their high-fives and hugs solve just about every problem a kid can have. And how adorable are little Michelle's catchphrases? "You got it, dude!" sounds just like something my adorable kids will say some day!

WHAT PARENTING IS ACTUALLY LIKE: *JUDGE JUDY*

If you have more than one child in your house, you need to ditch the high-fives and hugs and grab the judge's robe instead. Because that will be your primary role for the majority of your days. And Judge Judy has catchphrases that will come in handy a lot more often than Michelle Tanner's. One of her most relevant quotes is, "Don't pee on my leg and tell me it's raining." This works on a couple of levels, one being that kids make up elaborate stories and the other level being that kids also have a tendency to pee on you.

WHAT YOU THOUGHT PARENTING WAS GOING TO BE LIKE: *GREY'S ANATOMY*

Grey's Anatomy might not seem like a family show, but it does feature a lot of working women who happen to be moms. They are surgeons! Saving lives! And they are also great parents! See, you *can* do it all! At least, I think they are good parents. I'm not quite sure where their kids are most of the time. But look! Saving lives!

WHAT PARENTING IS ACTUALLY LIKE: COMPETITIVE COOKING SHOWS

Have you ever watched those cooking competitions in which people are running all around the set, grabbing various ingredients and pans, and putting out actual fires left and right? All the while the host and an audience are going back and forth between criticizing them and cheering them on? If you are a working mom, these shows look exactly like your average day. Except your average day involves a little more smoke and much less food pre-pared in anything that isn't a microwave.

WHAT YOU THOUGHT PARENTING WAS GOING TO BE LIKE: *GILMORE GIRLS*

Look at how Lorelai and Rory have it all together. Mother and daughter, bonding through witty banter and well-accessorized outfits!

WHAT PARENTING IS ACTUALLY LIKE: *WIPEOUT*

Wipeout is a show that features idiots trying to complete a ridiculous obstacle course, which has various elements meant to cause bodily harm to the participants. More often than not, the people on this show are taken out by large things that hit them violently in the head, causing them to be thrown to the ground. Very few make it to the finish line without permanent brain dam-age. This show is the best metaphor for parenthood that I've ever seen. Because parenting involves a lot more ass-kicking than witty banter.

WHAT YOU THOUGHT PARENTING WAS GOING TO BE LIKE: *MICKEY MOUSE CLUB*

This show wasn't so much about parenthood as it was about kids. It gave the impression that a group of children were capa-ble of things such as prolonged happiness and doing anything collaboratively. Look at all those kids singing and dancing in unison! Aren't children a delight?

WHAT PARENTING IS ACTUALLY LIKE: *UFC FIGHT NIGHT*

No, children aren't a delight. They are a cluster-f and they have turned your world, and more specifically your home, into one large cage match. The only thing they really do in unison is throw themselves on the ground and kick their feet, just like UFC fighters.

WHAT YOU THOUGHT PARENTING WAS GOING TO BE LIKE: *PARENTHOOD*

Now that I think about it, I may file suit against Lauren Graham for the constant lies her characters have told about parenting. In this show, several generations join together around the dinner table to eat and laugh while a heartwarming song plays. There is nothing their love and loyalty can't overcome. Sure, there are a lot of tears, but they are of the "We are so lucky and happy" variety.

WHAT PARENTING IS ACTUALLY LIKE: *THE AMAZING RACE*

A team of two sets off on a race around the world. In order to win they have to complete death-defying stunts, endure relationship-testing arguments, and eat a lot of cow testicles. The tears on this show are of the "I can't believe I just ate cow testicles and broke up with my spouse in a Taiwanese cab" variety. Watching this show is the best way to prepare for navigating a marriage after bringing kids into the picture.

WHAT YOU THOUGHT PARENTING WAS GOING TO BE LIKE: NATURE SHOWS (THE CUTE KIND)

Oh, my goodness! The mamma bear is cuddling her little cub so close! The baby tigers are so fluffy and cute! Nature is beautiful!

WHAT PARENTING IS ACTUALLY LIKE: NATURE SHOWS (THE REALISTIC ONES)

Oh, dear lord! What is that lion doing to that zebra?! Nature is so cruel!

Class dismissed.

I DON'T LIKE BABIES. Or more accurately, I don't know what to do with babies. They seem very breakable, their heads don't appear to be properly attached, and they have horrible conversation skills. When I go to visit a friend with a new baby, I have no instinct or desire to hold the child. What good could come of that, really? I could fumble the child, the child could spit up or pee on me, and most frighteningly of all I could accidently blurt out how unattractive and alienlike the baby is. It's just a bad idea all around.

Most of the time my aversion to babies doesn't cause much of an issue—as there are always plenty of other people who are ready and willing to fawn over the aliens. But this issue of mine can present a bit of a problem when the newborn is my own alien, because it's generally expected that a mother should know what the hell to do with her own child. The child itself is really banking on this fact.

When Vivian arrived I went through the motions of holding her, loving her, and breastfeeding her—as I was expected to do. But in reality I really had no idea what the hell I was doing. At least not at the beginning. I was overwhelmed by all the things I didn't know, all the instincts I was certain would never kick in. I was always scared I would accidently let her head roll off. I had trouble figuring out how to hold all seven pounds of her in a way that was anything less than completely awkward.

You know how actors look when they are pretending to be parents for a role and it's blatantly obvious that they have never actually held a child before? That's how I looked. Except this was real life and I really had a baby. No one was more alarmed by this plot development than I.

Over time I got the hang of it and eventually stopped feeling like Godzilla trying to operate a ChapStick every time I handled the baby.

But when Daniel came along the whole thing felt foreign again. It had been a couple of years since I'd held a newborn, and in that time I'd forgotten how it was done. He was so tiny and wobbly. But this time I made myself learn, instead of handing him off to Becky when I felt uncomfortable.

This time, instead of insisting that Becky stay awake our first night in the hospital, I encouraged her to get some sleep. After being awake for the twenty-four-hour birth, she gladly curled up on the room's ridiculously uncomfortable chair/bed and passed out.

The sun was down; the room was dark; all was quiet. And that's when I got to know Daniel.

I wasn't as unsure of myself this time around. I knew I knew how to do this, it was just a matter of reminding myself. So I held him and nursed him. I talked to him and moved around the room. And somewhere around 3:00 AM I remembered how to be a mom to a newborn.

I remembered where to put my arm and his head; I remembered how to swaddle him and change his diaper; I remembered how to breastfeed.

When Becky woke up in the morning and asked how everything went I looked at her and said, "We got this."

Now, obviously, not everything went smoothly simply because I remembered how to swaddle a baby. Shockingly enough, there is a little more to it than that. Spoiler alert.

Even though I had no idea what was coming my way as a mother of two children, at least this time I knew I was up to the task. I had developed my Mommy instincts over the last couple of years. They were well honed and unaffected by lack of sleep. They would guide me (often in a sleep-walking state) through this next phase of motherhood.

As you head out on your own adventure with Baby #2, it's important you also go into it with the confidence that you're prepared. You've been down this road before—or at least one with a very similar landscape. You know to expect quick turns and potholes along the way. And you've become very good at navigating it while half asleep. You got this.

They say that your heart grows in size with each of your children, but I don't think my heart grew. I think it was always this big; it was just waiting for these two to fill it up. My kids are like that time I trained for a marathon. I never thought I could survive even a mile, but then all of a sudden I was finishing 26.2. Who knew my heart and feet were capable of so much? (Let's not discuss my appearance after being exposed to either twenty-six miles or to parenthood because that would kill the positive vibe we've got going here.)

Yes, I'm comparing my two children to an endurance event that pushed me to my physical, emotional, and mental limits. Which isn't fair. Because my marathon had a finish line, and I'm in this race with these kids forever. Now that I think about it, I might need something stronger than ice and Advil during their teen years.

Just as when I was training for a marathon, there are miles of this parenting journey that aren't pretty. It's rare that I fall into bed at night and actually feel like I kicked the shit out of that particular day. In fact, usually it feels like I was on the bad end of the shit kicking.

But just as my marathon wasn't about one mile, parenting isn't about one moment. It's about all of the moments added up together into a messy, exhausting, exhilarating journey.

The moment you're breastfeeding Baby #2 at your toddler's Mommy and Me class and realize you forgot to change out of your spit-up-stained pajama top. Or the moment when you have to stop to get milk and both children have a meltdown for the entirety of the grocery store trip. And the moment when both kids get hit with the flu bug from hell twelve hours before you're scheduled to leave on a kid-free weekend getaway.

But the journey is also made up of moments when your toddler sleeps with your leg as a pillow while you cradle the new baby in your arms. And the moment one child jumps on your back while you chase the other around the house pretending to be a dragon. The never-ending noise of happy childhoods that fills your house. The look in their eyes when they spot you in the audience at their recital.

All these moments and a million more make up your messy, exhausting, exhilarating journey.

Be kind to yourself if not every moment fits into the exhilarating category. And accept early and often that perfect is not only unreasonable; it's ridiculous.

Your kids don't need perfect. They need a home that finds happiness in the chaos. One that errs on the side of laughter when the days go off-script. One where they know they're loved by the time that's spent with them, not by how many activities they have on their schedule or how elaborate their birthday parties are. And more than anything, your kids need to see in you what it means to be a happy adult. Giving them that example and that assurance is the greatest thing you can provide for them.

That means it's okay if you let yourself off the hook sometimes. Let your kids watch a little too much TV if you need their brains to shut down while you rest yours. Feed them chicken nuggets from the freezer every once in a while because sometimes you just need one thing in the day to be easy. If you miss a bath now and then, it's not the end of the world. And for the love of all that is pure, stay away from Pinterest. You don't need that kind of negative energy in your life.

Most important, always carve out a little time for yourself. Demand it the way you demand things for and from your children. Whether it be a ten-minute bath, a night out with friends, or a gym break, it's never selfish to refuel your soul. That fuel will make you better for everyone.

And be kind to the other moms you meet along this journey. Each of you is battling your own messy, exhausting, exhilarating children, and you'll be hard-pressed to find people who understand you better than those who are traveling the same route.

When you notice a mom who seems a little overwhelmed, give her a reassuring smile that tells her you've been there too. Maybe invite her to coffee or text her a picture of your chaotic life to assure her that she's not the only one whose house is an absolute disaster. Remind her, and yourself, that if you're worried about whether or not you're doing a good job, then you probably are doing a good job.

You are all fighting the good fight out there on the front lines. You are handling your cluster-f's with the love, patience, and resilience only a parent can summon day in and day out. And you also have plenty of wine, Nick Jr., and fruit snacks at the ready because you know that this battle is not for the ill prepared.

You got this, ladies.

Journal Entry
A LETTER TO DANIEL

Dear Daniel,

I gotta be honest, I had no idea how I was going to feel about you when you made your way out of my belly and into this world. I mean, I knew I would love you because I've loved you long before you arrived. I gave up caffeine for you, so my level of devotion should never be called into question.

But I was more concerned about whether I'd *like* you.

First of all, we all know how I feel about babies. Your sister had been out of that unfortunate stage for quite a while, and I found myself liking each advancing age more and more. She was bursting into childhood while you were going to be firmly rooted in the blob stage for some time. How on earth were you going to be able to compete with Queen Vivian the First in your state?

But then you made your appearance and I instantly knew I had just given birth to another love of my life. I know that sounds cheesy, but keep in mind I was heavily medicated. You had trouble taking your first breaths and the room was starkly quiet as we all waited for you to say hello. Then, because you were finally ready, you let out your first perfect baby cry. Your Mommy, Mama, and Grandma did a little crying too.

When I finally got to hold you I kept whispering in your ear, "I love you, buddy. You did such a good job. I'm so proud of you. You did such a good job." Over and over. I still grab you at least once a day and whisper, "I love you" in your ear before you wriggle away to your next adventure. Then and today I'm so proud of you for fighting to take that first little breath.

Although you were my second baby, this time it felt different. This time I wasn't crippled with fear because this time I knew I could take care of you. The greatest gift your sister ever gave you was teaching me how to be a mom, so that I didn't have to waste any of our first days together figuring it out.

Instead, you got a much calmer version of Mommy than Vivian was exposed to in the beginning. This Mommy didn't stress out when you kept her awake all night. This Mommy didn't spend nearly as much time on the Internet investigating all the ailments that could be affecting you at any given time. And this time Mommy even had professional newborn photos taken of you. (Vivian was six months old before Mommy got it together enough to send out birth announcements. People must have thought I had the longest gestation of all time.)

And you were different too. I'm not sure why I was expecting you to be exactly like the only other baby I had experienced, but most likely I was just hoping to avoid another treacherous learning curve. You had other ideas, however, and have spent most of your time paving a completely different path than that of your sister. And when I say "paving" I mean it in the way that the Tasmanian Devil "paves" a path. You were so much more relaxed than Vivian was as a baby—but then you made up for lost time by diving headfirst into your terrible twos at about thirteen months old. And most of the time you were literally diving headfirst.

While your sister has always been cautious and deliberate, you have proven to have little to no regard for the safety of any of your body parts. Your poor head seems to be the part you're the least concerned with. Since you started to walk you've always been on a quest to see how fast you can run and how high you can climb. Needless to say, you and gravity haven't been on the best of terms.

But then, in addition to your general disregard for the safety of your brain matter, you've always had the sweetest heart I've ever seen. You are quick to smile and give a bear hug with your tiny arms. You always take time out of your busy falling schedule to curl up on my lap for a while. When you were a little over two years old, there was a period of about three months when you told everyone in your life that you loved them about twenty times a day.

"Mommy, Mommy, Mommy!"

"Yes, Daniel?"

"I love you, Mommy!"

These days you prefer to grab our faces, plant a kiss right on our lips, lean in for a hug around the neck, and then announce, "I love you!" You have to do every step—each is equally important in your toddler mind. It's your version of a secret handshake, and I'm so lucky to be one of the people you've shared the code with.

The real reason I love hearing you say "I love you!" is because I know it wouldn't come off your lips so easily if it hadn't been picked up by your ears a million times. I'm so glad you know how adored you are and have always been, since that first time I whispered it in your ear.

We have a stuffed bear that we bought at one of your ultrasounds. When you press the bear's tummy it plays a recording of your heartbeat from when you were still in my belly. Hearing that heartbeat now takes me back to that time. It was a time when I was worried about what was to come. I was worried about how our family would accommodate another child—if we'd be able to do right by you and still keep up with Vivian.

Being Baby #2 can be hard. You were born into a family already in motion. But there will always be a place in my heart that is only yours. The place that holds all those quiet nights and stolen afternoons when just the two of us curled up on the recliner in your room for feedings. It also houses all the laughter, adventure, and excellent accessory choices you've brought into my life. It's the place that loves watching you grow into a person who is equally entertained running around with a bucket on his head or sitting for an hour doing complicated puzzles that are way beyond his age level.

And that corner of my heart will never forget the countless times you've proven over the years that not only could our family make room for another kid, but we weren't really complete until that other kid arrived.

You and your sister are loud and chaotic and exhausting. You have taken every aspect of my life and shaken it up like an Etch A Sketch. Sometimes I think you guys are holding secret meetings in your playroom, concocting elaborate plans on how to best break my brain.

But despite all of that, I love watching your sibling relationship unfold. The often messy beginnings of what I hope will become an anchor for both of you throughout your lives. You are already my anchors.

There is no greater joy in my life than when I get home and the two of you clamor across the room and crash into my arms, each of you yelling "Mommy!" as you bury your face into your side of my neck. You two fit perfectly there, like pieces I'd been waiting for. The pieces that made me whole.

ACKNOWLEDGMENTS

To my agents Lilly Ghahremani and Stefanie Von Borstel, for always having my back and doing all the lawyer-y stuff while I concentrate on coming up with new ways to describe baby vomit. To Seal Press, for allowing me to realize my dream of having a series of books with the word *Sh!t* in the title.

To Gail Marie Poverman-Kave (gailpovermankave.com), for once again offering some professional insight into my children's unstable brain matter.

To my Moms on the Front Lines (Brooke, Carrie, Colleen, Dana, Deanna, Deborah, Jen, Jill, Kaysee, Leah, Michaela, Michelle, Rachel, Sarah B., and Sarah G.), for providing their stories and support throughout the writing of all the *Sh!t* books. Whether or not I'm writing a book, they are quick with advice and humor. ("I'm pretty sure my toddler has rabies; it's the only logical conclusion. He even tried to bite my husband.") Their points of view add so much to the books, and I'm endlessly grateful for their honesty and hearts.

To Catherine Roe, for taking such good care of my babies three days a week. She started with us when Daniel was still a blob and has helped guide these two little people in so many ways.

To my parents, Betty Lou and Dave Dais, who are such a huge part of Daniel and Vivian's lives. I know from experience how lucky the kids are to have my parents in their corner.

To Becky Rook, for being there through all the sleepless nights, early mornings, dinnertime sing-alongs, bath-time protests, school pickups, toddler meltdowns—all the excruciatingly beautiful and alarmingly difficult parts of parenthood.

To Vivian Lucia and Daniel Paul, for your laughter, your energy, and your wide-eyed take on the world. For those magical mornings when we actually make it out of the house on time without any of us suffering a mental breakdown, the peaceful times you guys are in the general vicinity of each other and choose love instead of war, and for that one time you both ate what I made you for dinner.

Thank you.

There is no greater joy in my life than when I get home and the two of you clamor across the room and crash into my arms, each of you yelling "Mommy!" as you bury your face into your side of my neck. You two fit perfectly there, like pieces I'd been waiting for. The pieces that made me whole.

*D*AWN DAIS IS a freelance writer and graphic designer. Her previous books include *The Sh!t No One Tells You*, *The Sh!t No One Tells You About Toddlers*, and *The Nonrunner's Marathon Guide for Women*. She lives in Roseville, California, with her partner Becky, their kids Vivian and Daniel, their two very needy dogs, and their two rather moody cats. She is tired.

Stalk Dawn online at dawndais.com.

© JILLIAN GOULDING PHOTOGRAPHY

SELECTED TITLES FROM SEAL PRESS

The Sh!t No One Tells You: A Guide to Surviving Your Baby's First Year, by Dawn Dais. $16.00, 978-1-58005-484-3. A humorous, realistic, and supportive guide to the first 52 weeks with a baby by best-selling humor author—and new mother—Dawn Dais.

The Sh!t No One Tells You About Toddlers, by Dawn Dais. $16.00, 978-1-58005-589-5. Dawn Dais tells it like it is, again, offering real advice, hilarious anecdotes, and encouragement to help parents survive life with toddlers.

Here's the Plan: Your Practical, Tactical Guide to Advancing Your Career During Pregnancy and Parenthood, by Allyson Downey. $16.00, 978-1-58005-618-2. Offering advice on all practical aspects of ladder-climbing while parenting, such as negotiating leave, flex time, and promotions, *Here's the Plan* is the definitive guide for ambitious mothers, written by one working mother to another.

Raising the Transgender Child, by Michele Angello and Ali Bowman. $15.00, 978-1-58005-635-9. Written by top experts in the field, *Raising the Transgender Child* offers much-needed answers to all the questions parents and other adults ask about raising and caring for transgender and gender diverse children.

Please Don't Bite the Baby (and Please Don't Chase the Dogs): Keeping Your Kids and Your Dogs Safe and Happy Together, by Lisa Edwards. $16.00, 978-1-58005-577-2. Professional dog trainer Lisa Edwards offers prescriptive advice for families on bringing up baby with Fido in the home, and for bringing Fido home with kids in the house.

Not Buying It: Stop Overspending and Start Raising Happier, Healthier, More Successful Kids, by Brett Graff. $16, 978-1-58005-5918. In *Not Buying It*, Brett Graff, the "Home Economist," separates the truth about what parents need for their kids to succeed from the fiction perpetuated by ads, peer pressure, and internal fear.